301 Simple Things
You Can Do To Sell
Your Home NOW and
For More Money Than
You Thought

How To Inexpensively
Reorganize, Stage, and Prepare
Your Home For Sale

Revised 2nd Edition

Michael J. Cavallaro

301 SIMPLE THINGS YOU CAN DO TO SELL YOUR HOME NOW AND FOR MORE MONEY THAN YOU THOUGHT: HOW TO INEXPENSIVELY REORGANIZE, STAGE, AND PREPARE YOUR HOME FOR SALE - REVISED 2ND EDITION

Library of Congress Cataloging-in-Publication Data

Cavallaro, Michael J.
    301 simple things you can do to sell your home now and for more money than you thought : how to inexpensively reorganize, stage, and prepare your home for sale / Michael J. Cavallaro. -- 2nd edition.
        pages cm
    Earlier edition published in 2007 authored by Teri B. Clark.
    Includes bibliographical references.
    ISBN 978-1-62023-063-3 (alk. paper) -- ISBN 1-62023-063-1 (alk. paper) 1. House selling--United States--Handbooks, manuals, etc. I. Clark, Teri B. 301 simple things you can do to sell your home now and for more money than you thought. II. Title. III. Title: Three hundred one simple things you can do to sell your home now and for more money than you thought.
    HD259.C54 2015
    643'.120973--dc23

                                    2015018898

Printed on Recycled Paper

Reduce. Reuse.
RECYCLE.

A decade ago, Atlantic Publishing signed the Green Press Initiative. These guidelines promote environmentally friendly practices, such as using recycled stock and vegetable-based inks, avoiding waste, choosing energy-efficient resources, and promoting a no-pulping policy. We now use 100-percent recycled stock on all our books. The results: in one year, switching to post-consumer recycled stock saved 24 mature trees, 5,000 gallons of water, the equivalent of the total energy used for one home in a year, and the equivalent of the greenhouse gases from one car driven for a year.

Over the years, we have adopted a number of dogs from rescues and shelters. First there was Bear and after he passed, Ginger and Scout. Now, we have Kira, another rescue. They have brought immense joy and love into not just into our lives, but into the lives of all who met them.

We want you to know a portion of the profits of this book will be donated in Bear, Ginger and Scout's memory to local animal shelters, parks, conservation organizations, and other individuals and nonprofit organizations in need of assistance.

– Douglas & Sherri Brown,
President & Vice-President of Atlantic Publishing

Table of Contents

Chapter 5: Take the Home Out of the House 151

Introduction

You have a beautiful home or a not so beautiful home. Perhaps it is just an average home like the others in the neighborhood. The time has come to sell because you have a job in another city or have simply outgrown the space. Maybe you need to downsize since the children have moved out. Whatever the reason, you are putting your home on the market. You get a realtor or put up your "For Sale by Owner" sign and you wait. And wait. And wait.

Time goes by and you begin to think of reducing the price. More time goes by and you have found a new home, moved in, and have an empty house to sell and two mortgages, or your life is on hold and you wait some more. Why is your house taking so long to sell?

When asked this question, many people assume that market timing is poor or that the realtor is not doing a good job. They may even assume that the home is just "one of those homes" that no one really likes and will have to be reduced far below market value to move. In most cases these answers are far from the truth. The truth lies in home staging.

What is Home Staging?

According to one professional, "Staging helps realtors and home sellers prepare property for sale; the work I do reduces the number of days a home is on the market, attracts serious buyers, secures equity, and takes the stress out of selling." In the simplest sense, home staging is the art of preparing a home to sell. It is a combination of design, flow, and curb appeal. When a home has been staged it looks orderly, airy, full of light, and spacious. It looks salable. Staging is putting your best foot forward.

There are four things that affect the sale of your house:

- Location
- Market conditions

- Condition of your home
- Presentation of your home

There are some things that are out of your hands: you cannot change the location of your house or market conditions, but you can do something about the condition of your house and its presentation.

"Home staging" was coined by Barb Schwarz back in the early '70s. Ms. Schwarz currently runs a national training course on home staging at stagedhomes.com, and her site also offers a Top 15 stating tips for download. The concept of home staging has become well known as "house fluffing," "dressing to sell," and "home presentation" to name a few, but the concept has not taken hold among home owners when selling a home because many people do not understand the idea or need help to create a workable plan for staging their home correctly.

Home staging is more than just slapping a bit of paint on the wall or getting the odors out of the carpet. Both of these are just small pieces of the overall puzzle. Alone, they will not accomplish the goal of creating a notable first impression. As part of a whole, each home staging element will help your home sell faster and for more money.

Reality Check

One particular seller was not comfortable having her home staged. As with many sellers, she did not want her things rearranged. She did, however, let two rooms be staged for the purpose of getting professional photographs for the Web, albeit with express instructions to put everything back in its proper place after the photo session. Even after seeing the photos of her staged rooms, she was not sold on the process. She commented that the rooms looked bare.

For the next few weeks, each time the real estate agent showed the property, there would be fewer things lying around and each time something new would be done – throw pillows would be removed from the sofa, a favorite, but worn-out chair, would be hidden away, fresh flowers were placed on the dining room table instead of the placemats and newspapers, the dehumidifier was moved to a closet shelf, and the kitchen counters cleared.

It was obvious that the home owner was gradually staging her apartment. After several weeks, it almost looked as it did in the photos on the Web. A week later, the seller received an offer, which she accepted.

Are you listening to your stager or following the ideas in this book? If not, you are going to slow down the selling process.

You Get Only One Chance to Make a First Impression

That is right, you can sell your home faster AND for more money! How can that be? It all has to do with first impressions. Oh, I know that we have all been told not to judge a book by its cover, but doing so is just part of human nature.

First impressions are formed instantly. According to research done by Iowa State University, people are capable of taking in huge quantities of information in an instant – mostly as visual intake. A barrage of information including color, space, design, and size, congeals within 30 seconds into a favorable or unfavorable impression.

First impressions do not go away. Instead, people simply build on that impression during further encounters.

This Could Be You:
A Real Estate Agent Success Story

Someone I knew had just taken over as the head of a real estate development company in a suburban location. At the time, the market was somewhat depressed and his model homes were not selling. Given his marketing background, the first thing he did was to change his online listing. He tried web sites such as Zillow.com and Realtor.com, highlighted the unique features of the homes and showed floor plans so that buyers could get a really good feel for the properties.

Two weeks passed and although traffic to the model homes had increased, there were no sales. Next he increased his ad budget and put ads in local newspapers to try to reach more people. Again, he had no sales. Finally, he reduced prices, which of course he advertised, but that did not work either.

Completely mystified, he asked me to take a look at the models and give him my point of view. I told him that I thought the problem was quite simple   the homes were not staged. There was too much furniture, it was too dark and heavy for the space, and it was not properly placed. Consequently, prospective buyers could not get the full effect of the spaciousness of the homes and their wonderful and unique features.

With a warehouse of available furniture and a couple of assistants, I staged the model homes, using less furniture with better placement, and the right accessories, all to enhance the homes' spaciousness and best features. Immediately the homes began to sell.

For me, the most important aspect of this experience was that all the potential buyers who had been brought in through an expensive advertising campaign and then reduced prices were lost to the seller because the models did not look good to them. Had the homes been staged FIRST before spending on advertising or price reductions, profits would have been higher.

You have only one chance to make a good first impression.

Real estate agents are well aware of this phenomenon, even if they cannot quote the latest statistics. Having carefully researched homes and made appointments to view these homes with a prospective buyer, agents often feel frustrated when the buyer will not even get out of the car because they "do not like the look of the front." It is not easy to overcome these first impressions. Once they are made, you will be fighting against them every step of the way.

In its 2014 annual survey of home buyers, the National Association of Realtors found that 92 percent of buyers use the internet for their home search process and 50 percent of buyers use a mobile website or application in their home search. Realtor.com, one of the most popular online sites, offers a mobile app for download on Windows Store, Apple's App Store, and on Google Play. Mobile apps are playing an increasing role due to the fact that people access tend to access additional real estate information while visiting other homes in the surrounding area. If they visit a home within five miles of your posting, and decide they don't like the listing, they will call up additional listings on their mobile app and see your listing. Thanks to these apps, prospective buyers now have the same access to listings of homes as real estate agents. The contents of multi-listing services, once closely guarded by real estate agents, is now readily available on the Internet. Access has tilted the market structure to favor buyers who know what you have for sale before you know that they want to buy. Search engines such as Google make it easy for to gather all kinds of community information, thus reducing buyers' buyers dependence on realtors. According to eBizMBA.com, the top 15 most popular real estate web sites (ranked by Quantcast according to estimated monthly visitors) are:

1. www.zillow.com
2. www.trulia.com
3. www.homes.yahoo.com
4. www.realtor.com
5. www.www.redfin.com
6. www.homes.com
7. www.apartmentguide.com
8. www.curbed.com
9. www.remax.com
10. www.hotpads.com
11. www.ziprealty.com
12. www.apartments.com
13. www.rent.com

14. www.auction.com

15. www.forrent.com

Prospects are now capable of handing the real estate agent a list of what they want to see before the real estate agent's list is even out of the drawer. These prospective buyers go into a home – your home   and instantly form an emotional reaction to what they see and feel. One misplaced picture or one too many pieces of furniture can sound the instant death knell of interest.

This Could Be You:
A Real Estate Agent Success Story

I sold a home while it was being staged. A buyer, unaware that we were there staging, come in and saw the home partially staged. She wanted to come back the next day with her family. When she brought them back, we were finished. She said, "I have to make a contract on this home. As beautiful as it looks, it will get picked up fast." And she bought the furniture, too!

Prospects know there are alternatives and will quickly be off to the next home on their list. Over time this can produce your worst nightmare   an empty house. An empty house gives off a distressed feel   a sense that you may dump the property fast and cheap. Ironically, buyers have more difficulty visualizing life in an empty house, perhaps explaining the greater difficulty of selling them. Since the average buyer sees 10 homes in 10 weeks, according to The National Association of Realtors, you need to do something to make your home stand out from the rest of the crowd.

That is why making a good first impression can make all the difference. It would be a wise decision to present your home in its best light from the start.

CASE STUDY

The job of a real estate agent is to convince the seller that staging a home works.

A stager sells a dream. Those who buy a home are looking for the dream home. They want to visualize themselves in a home feeling happy. In the world today, families are busy, busy, busy. That is why it is essential to have a home that feels calm. I always try to have a space that has no TV or computer and instead has a couple of chairs and a chessboard to give the buyer the idea that they will be able to sit as a family and enjoy the home. That is what they are seeking: a home in which they can have a happy, contented life. What do you see when you go into a display home? It gives you a feeling that life is in control and complete. That is the feeling that you need to create in the seller's home.

Square footage used to be the standard for selling a home. People used to look at a home and think, "What can I do with this house?" All that has changed.

People do not think in square feet anymore. They look at the way the house is laid out and arranged. They want something that they can live in right now. They have busy lives and do not want to hassle with renovating or making changes. They work two jobs and have children and do not want unfinished things that add more stress to their lives. They go with the house they can see themselves living in.

That is why staging is a combination of seduction and competition. It is all about the buyer and not the seller   the hardest concept to get through to sellers! They want to show off their things, their good taste, and what they have done to the house. The only way to stage a home properly, however, is to help the seller give up those emotional ties.

Many sellers do not want to put any money into the home they are selling. They want to sell it "as is." However, putting just a bit of money into it can result in a higher return. If money or time is truly a constraint, then concentrate on the living room, kitchen, master bedroom, and master bath. Leave the rest to the imagination of the buyer.

Proper staging may be inconvenient for sellers. They have to do work. They have to change how the house is arranged. They have to live in a home but have it look as though it is not lived in. I always remind them, however, that it is all about selling the house – always keep that goal in mind. It is big work, but it is worth it and it will pay off. Home staging is not just someone's opinion. It works.

A True Life Example

If you doubt that putting work into an "impression" will make any difference to the home buyer, I can prove to you that it does.

Have you ever toured a model home in a development or a home manufacturer's show lot? Let us think about what you see when you arrive. All the paint is fresh. All the fixtures and appliances sparkle. The artwork is pretty and there are fresh flowers or bowls of fruit on the counter and tabletop. The bathroom is something to behold with fresh towels and shiny mirrors. There is no clutter: no children's toys, no piles, nothing to catch your attention except the beauty of the home. The house simply looks beautiful and spacious and comfortable. It gives you the feeling that you should move in right away.

Now, let us contrast this with a typical home in the same development that has been lived in for the last five years. The paint is five years old and has smudges and fingerprints. Fixtures and appliances no longer shine. They look old, and the refrigerator handle has a dark area from grimy fingers. Walls are covered in family photos, and countertops hold every latest kitchen gadget as well as a pile of bills. The bathroom, although clean, has mismatched towels draped over the shower curtain rod and on the back of the door. There are toothpaste spatters on the mirror. Toys and other personal belongings are scattered here and there throughout the home. All the furniture and the "stuff" make the rooms feel small and cramped. The house says "lived in" – lived in by someone else.

You be the judge. Which house is more appealing to you? Of course, it is the model home. No, it is not the way you would have the home if you lived there, but it is the way you want to see it so that you can envision living there. The model home was prepared to show off all the good features and none of the bad ones.

The Stats Tell the Whole Story

Statistics gathered by StagedHomes.com show that proper home stage training can sell homes in as little as 11 days and for 17 percent higher than the original listing price! In some areas, that number can go as high as 50 percent! These statistics also show that homes that had not sold in an average of four and a half months after listing sold within a week of being staged by a professional. Homes that were staged before listing were under contract more than twice as fast as comparable homes that had not been professionally staged. Staging your home will put "SOLD" on the sign. Plus, less marketing time equals less seller stress.

"I have seen the reaction to a well staged home as well as one that is not staged," said one professional. "Buyers mentally dismiss a house when they see how much time and work they will have to devote to it before moving in. Selling your home 'as is' only helps the competition! Get buyers competing to buy your house so you do not have to take the first low ball offer you get. The longer it stays on the market the more stigmatized your house will be, and people look at days on market when deciding on the offer. Get the buzz going from the start!"

For example, if you have your home on the market for four and a half months and have house payments of $1,000, you will put another $4,500 into your home before the sale. Since you had your home on the market for so long, you will most likely have lowered the price or be willing to accept a lower offer. Let us assume that you wanted $250,000 and were willing to settle for $239,000. That is another $11,000, for a total loss of $15,500.

Consider the home staged house. You will only be there one month, so you only have to make one house payment of $1,000. You spend $750 on the staging process and $1,000 for one month's housing expenses. However, because you staged your home, you ask 17 percent more than you would have for a sale price of $292,500. Minus the $750 for staging and $1,000 for one's month's living expense, you end up making $40,750 instead of losing $15,500. So, instead of selling your non-staged home for $239,000, you stage everything and sell it for $292,500 a difference of $53,500. Certainly, these numbers catch your attention.

This Could Be You:
A Real Estate Agent Success Story

When people say that they want to sell their home for the most money possible, most would be satisfied to get their asking price. What would you think of getting $100,000 OVER your asking price? That happened to one realtor's clients. After staging the home, it sold in just two weeks for $699,000 instead of the asking price of $599,000. According to Donna, staged homes get more than the asking price all the time!

Keep in mind that this example used the lowest possible increase in price. Although the average home is more likely to sell at 6 percent to 8 percent more, the percentage increase in staging can range anywhere between 6 and 20 percent. Looking at the table below, you can get a feel for the price increase when selling a staged house. There is simply no need to turn down extra money.

Unstaged	Staged 6 percent	Staged 8 percent	Staged 17 percent	Staged 20 percent
$100,000	$106,000	$108,000	$117,000	$120,000
$125,000	$132,500	$135,000	$146,250	$150,000
$150,000	$159,000	$162,000	$175,500	$180,000
$200,000	$212,000	$216,000	$234,000	$240,000
$250,000	$265,000	$270,000	$292,500	$300,000
$300,000	$318,000	$324,000	$351,000	$360,000
$400,000	$424,000	$432,000	$468,000	$480,000
$500,000	$530,000	$540,000	$585,000	$600,000
$1 million	$1.06 million	$1.08 million	$1.07 million	$1.2 million

PROFESSIONAL BONUS TIP:

Home staging is such a bargain. The return on the money is phenomenal. The service that the stager supplies to the client can yield them $10 on the $1 for a lived-in house. You can get a home staged for $600 to $1,200 and that boosts your asking price at least $6,000 to $12,000 or more.

Professional or Do-It-Yourself?

You have the option of choosing a professional or going it alone. Do you get a mechanic when your car breaks down? It depends on your knowledge of car repair and the extent of the problem. Your decision about your house is based on your comfort level.

Something to consider when deciding if you should use a professional is whether you can detach yourself from your home and see it as a house. Did you realize that you are not selling your home? You are selling a house to someone who will turn it into their home. From the moment that you decide to put your home on the market, it stops being your home and becomes someone else's dream.

The memories you have of your home will not show up in the house you sell. Prospective buyers who come into your home do not care one iota about your memories. They are concerned about their hopes and dreams and how this house will fulfill them. The goal in presenting your home for sale is to have nothing interfere with potential buyers' imagining living there.

Buyers coming through the doors today want to see what their new home will be like. They are busy visualizing how it fits their needs rather than assessing how nice this stranger's house looks. They are checking to see if their furniture will fit, determining eating arrangements, considering traffic patterns, deciding where to hang the family heirloom, and a myriad of other things. They will not be able to do this if you insist on selling a home and not a house. If they cannot visualize themselves creating their own home, you will lose the sale.

Staging your own home means that you will have to see your home through the eyes of the buyer. The marks on the wall showing the heights of your children are not likely to be viewed fondly by potential buyers. They will simply see dirty walls. The fireplace mantel covered with family photos is not likely to create a loving smile either. They will just see crowded space where their things will never fit. Home stagers can be important because, often, new eyes are necessary. We get immune to our stuff. Home stagers have a fresh eye.

Preparing your home for sale can be challenging. This is not to say that you cannot stage your own home, because you can. You just have to understand what it takes to do so.

Reality Check

Surprises can be really fun – like a surprise birthday party. However, some surprises are not pleasant, like walking into a room full of birds. Not stuffed birds or decorative birds, but real live birds. The room was filled with birds that were flying loose, while others squawked in their cages. As you can imagine, the birds were not potty trained and the room was a disgusting mess. A surprise like this can kill a sale!

Is there anything about your home that might provide a nasty surprise to a buyer? Pets are often the culprit, but it can also be odors, colors, or even sounds.

Effort, Time, and Money – In That Order

Effort, time, and money are listed in the order of importance. It will take effort on your part to stage your home. If you do it yourself, the effort will be focused on seeing your home through the buyer's eyes. You will have to be able to find the things in your home that will be seen as defects. Then you will have to eliminate them.

Even if you choose to get a professional, the effort required will be great. You will have to make an effort to listen to their professional wisdom without getting your feelings hurt. Remember – staging is not decorating. When a home stager asks you to remove photos or pictures on the wall, she is not suggesting that you have poor taste. She simply knows her trade and knows what sells.

The time it will take to stage your home depends on the size of your home, how much needs to be done, and how quickly you work! For some people, a few hours will do a world of good. For most homes, count on a week or two.

Finally, consider money. One of the objectives of home staging is to make more money on your house. For example, you have a $150,000 home. According to the research, the minimum you stand to make by home staging is $4,500. But if you spend $4,000 making improvements, you really only get a $500 return. That is not much money for the effort and time required, is it?

Staging should not be expensive. Hiring a professional should not cost more than a few hundred dollars plus the cost of the supplies and materials to make the changes. Doing it yourself should cost even less – that is, if you truly follow professional staging rules. If not, you will waste time and money trying to do a professional job and, in the end, need to hire a professional to come in and do it right. If you are selling your home, professional home staging may just be the best short-term investment you can make!

CASE STUDY

Why is it that sellers do not want to spend any money on a house that they are leaving, yet will live in the house for months paying mortgage and even reduce the price tens of thousands of dollars? Do not be penny wise and pound foolish!

Staging is not the only place where sellers are pound foolish. The same applies to repairs. It is essential and needs to be done before putting the house on the market. Think about it this way: would you sell a car with a flat tire?

People take the idea of staging personally. Remember, it is not about your personal taste. It is about research and what this research shows. It is about marketing your house and doing what it takes to get it to sell. It is not about your home, but it is about a house. Specifically, it is about what can sell your house.

There is no real difference between what I suggest for modest homes and expensive homes, or small homes and large homes. I would even offer the same suggestions for mobile homes and condominiums. I simply make recommendations based on the expectations of the house. For instance, granite counters need to be in granite-counter neighborhoods. You need to match what is expected in that price range and in that area.

Keep in mind that there are many things that look expensive but are not! You only need the accessories to last six weeks and then your house is sold!

The idea of matching also applies to more modest homes. You would not suggest that a modest home in a modest neighborhood add granite countertops if the other houses in the neighborhood do not have them and the people looking at the home will not be expecting to find them.

If at all possible, do not show an empty house. People cannot conceptualize the scale. If they go into a huge bedroom, they will assume it is smaller than it really is. They will have trouble believing that their bedroom furniture can really fit in the room. You will need to put something in certain rooms to help them conceptualize the scale. Leave the cozy chair and an end table with a pillow in the living room to give a taste of what the room could be as well as the scale of the room. Put a card table and chairs with a long tablecloth over the table and slipcovers over the chairs under the chandelier in the dining room. Help the buyers see the potential of the room.

I sometimes bring in my own props for both occupied and vacant homes. These props include artwork and large-scale accessories because, in general, people do not have them. I have even created slipcovers for dining room chairs or other furniture that has the right size but is either too dingy or the wrong color.

Many people, when trying to stage on their own, depersonalize too much and create a boring a sterile space. If everything is off the counter in the kitchen, people will think, "Can anyone cook in here?" It is not inviting. Put some personality back in to make your home memorable and to allow the buyers to imagine themselves living there.

Staging is about selling your home quickly and for the best price possible. Do not let a small upfront investment keep you from having your own home-selling success story.

What You Will Learn from this Book

Whether you choose to stage your home yourself or hire a professional, understanding these techniques will help guide you along the home-selling and staging journey. You need to have more than the general idea of "fix it up and make it look better." What are you going to do specifically? Are you going to paint? Put in flowers? Add shutters? Change the carpet? You need an actual working list to check off instead of just winging it.

And that is why this book was written – to give you, the home seller, the knowledge to increase the value of your home and sell your home faster.

In the following pages you will learn how to:

- Remove the clutter to add space and flow
- Depersonalize your home so that a buyer can visualize how it will look with their own possessions
- Deep clean your home to make it shine like new
- Recognize the needed repairs that could cost a sale
- Determine when a true remodel job is needed
- Create curb appeal for a lasting first impression
- Add light to create enticing, airy spaces
- Home stage even if you do not have much money to spend on the venture
- Add small touches that will bring in big profits
- Make your home inviting for open houses and showings

Staging is not the same as interior decorating. Do not confuse the two. They are different. The focus of staging is to make a home more marketable by creating the home to appeal to the greatest number of prospective buyers. It should be impersonal enough not to infringe on a buyer's own sense of style.

Decorating is optional. Staging is essential – that is if you want to sell your house for the most possible money in the shortest amount of time. Staging is the difference between ordinary and extraordinary.

Are you ready to embark on the home staging journey? Here we go!

Getting Started TIPS

1. Think of staging as a risk-free proposition. If you do not like what you see, you can always change it back!

2. Staging your home will cost you LESS than your first price reduction!

3. Stage your home to have that competitive edge. This will result in achieving top dollar.

4. A stager's job is to make your home look like a model home. Home staging is not about decorating; it is about showcasing your house instead of your things!

5. The preparation for the first impression is the time before prospective buyers ever arrive. The time is now. You only get one chance to make a great first impression.

6. Be sure that your home is staged before you or your realtor takes photos for real estate Web sites like Zillow or Trulia. More than 70 percent of all new apartment/home searches are started on the Internet. It is imperative that the property look good in the photos so that it can attract as many people as possible to see the real thing.

7. You should not have one person look at your house until it has been staged completely. It should not go through the broker walkthrough, Realtor.com, open houses, or anything. Stage first!

8. When staging your own home, you will be forced to view your home critically and leave all the fond memories for your scrapbook.

9. If you find that staging your home is taking too long, revisit your plan of action and see if you are doing more than staging and have gone into revamping the whole house. Revamping is not the key. The way to get the most out of staging is to do as little as possible for the biggest "WOW" factor.

10. Always weigh the benefits against the costs before deciding on any large-scale projects.

11. Many people are willing to have their home appraised but not spend money on staging it. In reality, it would be better to have your home staged first and then appraised. Appraisers are also affected by psychology and will see a staged home as a better quality home than an unstaged one.

12. According to the National Association of Realtors (NAR), the average staging investment is between 1 and 3% of the home's asking price, which generates a return of 8 to 10%.

Chapter 1

Repair It and Refresh It

T he time has come to sell your home. You are ready to put the sign in the front yard. Or are you? Take a look around. Do you see anything amiss?

We often live in a house for years walking around the squeaky step or just knowing that the doorbell does not ring. We learn from experience that the light switch in the garage only works when you wiggle it, and the garbage disposal sounds like a freight train. This may seem insignificant to you, but it will not be insignificant to a buyer.

Even the tiniest of maintenance problems evokes a sense of fear in the potential buyer. A small water leak? That could be a sign of bigger problems.

Perhaps the roof leaks. Or there are huge plumbing problems. And thus their minds race – directly toward another house for sale.

Home repairs also conjure up the idea of work. Few people looking for a new home are also looking for "home work." They want to buy a home, relax, entertain, and live. They cannot do these things if they are working on the home and spending money on the repairs.

When you are selling your home, what you consider to be little annoyances can turn into big issues. That is why you must stop ignoring them and repair them.

PROFESSIONAL BONUS TIP:

Do not offer money toward painting or installing new carpeting. Remember, if you are not willing to do it, your buyer is not likely to either.

CASE STUDY

One time I was showing a home owner her newly staged master bedroom. It had been extremely cluttered with large unmatched, outdated furniture, too many personal items, and knickknacks. Even the TV was old and had been sitting on a scuffed dresser because it wasn't a flat screen that could be mounted on the wall.

After removing or rearranging the furniture, window treatments, and accessories, the room looked significantly better and larger, but the old dresser had been removed and there was no place for the TV. Since the house was being staged in time for an upcoming open house, we put the TV temporarily into the walk-in closet. The home owner was so excited at the transformation of the bedroom that she said she was going to keep the TV in the in closet and her husband could watch it in there!

This type of reaction is typical when home owners see what staging can do for their home. Regardless of size or price, all types of homes can benefit from staging because people set up their homes and live in them based on functionality, comfort, and their own sense of aesthetics. This is rarely suitable when selling a property. By staging an apartment or home, the "personal" aspect is neutralized so that it will appeal to a much wider range of people. Staging enhances the most positive features of the house, while the negative ones are minimized.

One of the biggest hurdles I have to overcome with home owners is their resistance to taking personal objects down and packing them away while the home is up for sale. Whether it is family photos, unique collections, or just personal mementos, home owners become emotionally attached and often do not want to live without these objects.

The other hurdle is that sellers believe that home staging is only for properties that are "taste-challenged." If they believe that their home is decorated in good taste or if it has been professionally designed, they think that it will not need to be staged. But you do not want buyers focusing on décor (especially if their style preference is different from the seller's). You want them to see the space. Plus, there are few homes or apartments that could not benefit from removing clutter.

While the furnishings, accessories, and finishes may be of a higher quality for expensive properties, the process is the same. Staging is about putting a home, regardless of price, in its best "showcase condition" to sell it for the most amount of money in the least amount of time.

Staging is absolutely a must in vacant homes and apartments. Although it is counter intuitive, homes and apartments look smaller when they are empty. Add the realization that many buyers are not able to visualize furniture arrangements or flow, and you will realize that vacant homes need to be staged.

Therefore, it is important to furnish and accessorize them to accomplish three things:

1. Make the space feel larger

2. Show buyers possible furniture placement (and whether their king size bed can really fit in the master bedroom!)

3. Give the property a warmer, more inviting feel so that a buyer can make that all important "emotional" connection

Whenever possible, I enjoy working with the furniture and accessories that a seller already has in their home. Sometimes that may mean moving furniture from one room to another or displaying one large item in place of several smaller ones. Other times it may be necessary to bring in some furniture or accessories to add to what they have or in place of some of their pieces to achieve the overall look.

It is important to repair items in your home. The most essential repairs fall into two categories. Repairs in the first category are those that are extremely visible such as cracks in the walls or ceilings, broken windows, and peeling paint. Even if they would be inexpensive for a buyer to fix, prospective buyers will view these small issues as a home that is not well maintained and that may have many other "hidden" problems as well.

Repairs in the second category are those that affect functionality such as leaky faucets and loose door handles. You do not want buyers to be focusing on these defects; they should be focusing on all the positive features of the home.

For most staging projects there is no time to do renovations. The property needs to go on the market "immediately" and renovations, especially those that would require professional help, take a lot of time. If the home owners are willing to do some work themselves, it is possible to lay a new floor in a room, pull up carpeting, sand and polish wood floors, or replace cabinet doors in the kitchen fairly quickly.

Even though it may seem time-consuming, renovations can boost a home's value and should be done if the home is in poor shape or completely outdated, or in a room such as the kitchen or bath, where the return on investment (both time and money) will pay off. It is critical to remember that any renovations should be done in as neutral a style as possible since the goal is to appeal to as many buyers as possible. Buyers do not want to pay extra for a newly renovated kitchen that simply is not their taste.

The best, easiest, most inexpensive, and least time-consuming renovation is paint. A light and neutral background is the perfect backdrop and can totally transform a property.

Transforming your home into a showcase   one that excites the buyers and helps the home or apartment sell quickly for the most money – is the goal of staging.

The Easiest and Least Expensive Way to Add Pizzazz to Your Home – Paint!

According to every real estate agent, home designer, home redecorator, and home stager I have ever spoken with, paint is the one thing that can make the most difference in a home. Paint makes a home look fresh and new on the inside and never fails to impress. It can be your best investment when selling your home.

This Could Be You:
A Real Estate Agent Success Story

In a big booming area in an older part of town sat a gorgeous, 20-year-old home. It backed up to a lake and had a well-developed lot. The home had three decks in the back to enjoy the view. It was competing with new homes and had sat for nearly a year quite unusual for the area. They were moving to Florida, and their new home had already been built. They were paying two mortgages and could not understand why their house would not sell.

A neighbor recommended that they contact me, and the owners were willing to try anything. I walked inside and immediately knew the problem. Although well built and beautiful in its day, it was too dark. The home had wainscoting, baseboards, and double trim crown molding all dark. Twenty years ago, it was prime. Now it was not. I asked them if they really meant that they would do anything, and they affirmed they would. I had them paint every piece of trim in the house a lovely, glossy, rich ivory color. I also helped them with a bit of staging by getting rid of family pictures and taking out dated furniture. Additionally, they had an odd room that just did not seem to have a function, so I designated it as an office to give the buyer a way to use the space. The total investment was $6,000, and their home sold in two weeks. Six thousand dollars is not that much money when you get your asking price in two weeks. It is far cheaper than paying two mortgages for months!

It is not an expensive operation and often you can do it yourself. Be sure not to choose colors based on your own preferences but based on what would appeal to the widest possible number of buyers. You should almost always choose an off-white color because white helps your rooms appear bright and spacious. However, to keep your home from feeling humdrum, you can use other neutral tones as well such as yellows, blues, and creams.

PROFESSIONAL BONUS TIP:

Be willing to change paint colors. There are certain universally accepted colors that should be used when repainting your home. Yellow or shades of gold are warm and inviting. You should also accent with yellow. Yellow is eye-catching.

Patching drywall

Or course, before you can paint, you will need to fix any holes in the drywall. Here is how:

1. Clear away any raised pieces of drywall paper around the edge of the hole.
2. Sandpaper all around the edges of the hole to roughen the paint.
3. If the whole is one to three inches wide, you can apply self-adhesive plastic mesh tape to it.

4. Use a putty knife to apply spackling compound to the hole. Make sure it is as smooth as possible. Reapply after the first spackling layer shrinks.

5. Allow the spackling to dry.

6. Sand the area smooth.

7. Prime and paint.

8. If the hole is larger, find the stud that is closest to the hole and use a knife or saw to cut out a rectangle drywall around the area. Be sure to include half the width of the stud so that the patch can be attached later.

9. Use sandpaper to roughen around the edges.

10. Cut a new piece of drywall the same size as the hole you cut out.

11. Attach the new drywall patch to the stud using drywall screws or drywall nails. Be careful not to break the paper by setting the heads too deep.

12. Using a putty knife, apply a thin coat of joint compound along the seams. Press paper joint tape into the joint compound. Make sure the edges of the tape are in the compound, but scrape away any excess.

13. After that coat dries, apply two more thin coats over the tape, extending several inches on each side to blend into the original wall.
14. Sand lightly between coats.
15. Prime the new patch.

Now it is time to paint.

How to prepare a room for painting

Painting is not difficult, but there are specific steps to follow for good results. The best results happen because of good preparation.

> **Step 1.** Remove all the furniture you can. For those pieces that cannot be moved out of the room, move them into the center and cover them and the floor with drop cloths. Use removable (usually blue) "safety" masking tape to shield moldings, doors, and windows.
>
> **Step 2.** Cover the smoke detector with a plastic bag and turn off air conditioning or heating while sanding or painting.
>
> **Step 3.** Sand or scrape loose flaky paint with sandpaper and paint scrapers – down to bare surfaces if necessary.

PROFESSIONAL BONUS TIP:

Sometimes, no amount of scraping and sanding will smooth a wall. If you have walls that are rough, consider putting a faux finish on them to hide little flaws.

> **Step 4.** Using a putty knife, fill all nail and screw holes with spackling compound and fill cracks with caulk.

Step 5. Wash all surfaces with trisodium phosphate (TSP) to remove grease and dirt. Use paint deglosser on glossy surfaces such as trim.

Step 6. Rinse everything well with water to remove the TSP. Allow surfaces to dry thoroughly and then dust and vacuum as needed.

Step 7. Turn off the power to the room and remove the cover plates from all electrical fixtures, outlets, and switches. Place small bits of masking tape over switch handles and outlets to protect them from paint. It is safest to leave the power off as you paint the room. If you decide to turn the power back on, work carefully around electrical areas.

Step 8. Loosen or remove cover plates from light fixtures; cover what remains with plastic bags. Remember not to turn on the lights because melting plastic really stinks.

Step 9. Remove heating and air-conditioning vent covers.

Painting techniques

Before you actually begin painting, you need to decide on the finish. The various finishes are flat, matte, satin, semi-gloss, and gloss. Each is intended for particular uses.

Here are a few tips and tricks for painting your walls that will help you do so in a professional manner.

- Paint the ceiling first, followed by walls and then the trims and moldings.

- Holding a small container of paint in one hand makes painting faster.
- Avoid drips by not overloading the roller or brush.
- Use a narrow brush for trims and an angled brush to fill "cut-in" edges.
- Be sure to clean your brushes after work outdoors. Water-soluble latex paint in the brush can be rinsed thoroughly in running water. Blot the water with paper towels and keep brushes in a plastic wrap. You may need to use turpentine oil to clean oil or alkyd paints from the brush or roller.

Do not forget to paint your ceilings. However, if you have a texture-sprayed ceiling, you will not be able to use a roller. Rolling popcorn ceilings can pull off the texture and leave bare spots. Spraying is the best option.

If you do decide to use a roller, you will want to do the following:

- Choose a roller made for rough surfaces
- Be gentle
- Place a drop cloth underneath the area you are painting to catch the popcorn that falls off

Strip Off the Years

When it comes to wallpaper, it is amazing how tastes change. What is "in" today is "out" tomorrow. If you have not kept up with the latest fashion, your home may be out of date. Can you imagine trying to sell this house? Duck murals went out in the '70s.

Although you may not have anything as drastic to remove, you will want to look over your wallpaper choices with a critical eye. Anything that is too busy, too bold, or too out-dated should probably go.

PROFESSIONAL BONUS TIP:

Wallpaper needs to be stripped since it Is easily dated. It is more like clothing. My suggestion is that 99 percent of the time it needs to come down.

Before you begin the process, you need to identify the type of wall paper and what kind of walls you have. The age of the wall determines whether it is drywall or plaster. Plaster is found mostly in homes that are more than 50 years old. In plaster walls, wood lath is nailed to wood-framed walls and covered with two or three coats of plaster. These walls are more solid and sound dull if you knock on them.

Drywall - It's been used in homes for the past 50 years or so. Drywall is a sheet of chalk-like substance covered with a lightweight cardboard. These sheets are nailed over wood-framed walls and have a hollow sound when you knock on them. Drywall is more delicate than plaster, so be careful not to damage the cardboard facing when using a wallpaper scraping tool.

If you have at least one room of wallpaper that needs to come down, here is an easy way to accomplish the task.

1. As much as is practical, cover the floor and furniture with drop cloths, old sheets, or discarded blankets. It is

Duck mural from the '70s

a good idea to move the furniture into the center of the room to make it easier to cover.

2. Start in any corner and try to peel the wallpaper off with your hands or use a putty knife or a wallpaper scraper.

3. If the paper does not peel off or if peeling the paper leaves behind the wallpaper's backing, it is time to get out the serious tools: razor blades. Be really careful not to cut into the drywall underneath.

4. If the wallpaper is stubborn and will not come off, the next step is to wet the wall. You can use plain water, a commercial wallpaper remover, or water mixed with dishwashing liquid. Apply the water with a paint roller, squirt gun, or a sponge. Just keep wetting the wall until the glue behind the wallpaper begins to loosen.

5. Try to peel the paper again using your hands, a putty knife, or a scraper.

6. Use a large sponge or scouring pad to clean any remaining glue from the wall. You want to have the wall stripped down completely before painting or putting up new wallpaper.

7. If there is glue remaining, let the wall dry. Then use coarse sandpaper to sand off any remaining glue or backing.

PROFESSIONAL BONUS TIP:

If the wallpaper is in good shape and is not peeling or separating at the seams, you can simply paint over it. Do not try to paint over flocked paper or paper with a raised design. Or, you can go to Home Depot or Loews and buy a wallpaper removal tool, such as a wallpaper steamer, liquid or gel remover. Liquid gel removers require that you score or scratch the wallpaper before application, but both removers contain wetting agents that dissolve old adhesive. Gels are especially effective for unprimed drywall and are less mess than liquids, and they liquefy the adhesive without softening or soaking the face of the drywall. Steamers are more effective than both gels and liquids, but they can be expensive pieces of machinery, so if gels and liquids do not work, consider renting one instead of buying it.

Add a Bit of Flair

As I said, wallpaper styles come and go, making it best to replace a wall-papered wall with nothing more than paint, but if you are determined to put wallpaper back up, find a pattern that is not distracting to the eye and is not too busy.

Hanging wallpaper is a bit trickier than removing it, but with these steps you will be able to handle the job yourself.

Preparing the Walls

1. Look for cracks, nail holes, loose paint, or plaster on the walls. Fix them before hanging the wallpaper.

2. Be sure that the walls are clean and dry and that every surface is either painted or primed. You do not want to apply paste to a surface that will just absorb it. The paper might not stick.

3. Remove all the electrical plates AFTER you have washed the walls. You do not want to get an electric shock!

4. Plan to start papering in a place that is inconspicuous and remember that your starting point will also be your ending point.

5. Beginning at a doorway or corner, measure a distance an inch or two shorter than the width of your paper. Make a small mark. Be sure to make the mark as light as possible so that it will not show through the paper's background.

6. Using a carpenter's level and a pencil, draw a vertical line from the floor to the ceiling through the two marks. If you start at a corner, be sure to use the level, not the corner, as your guide. You will

align your paper to this line. Again, be sure to make the mark as light as possible.

Hanging the Paper

1. With a utility knife, cut a length of paper that is about four inches longer than the wall is high from baseboard to ceiling. (With a large repeating pattern, you might have to cut the strips longer to make sure the pattern matches up from piece to piece.)

2. Apply paste to the paper, or if using prepasted wallpaper, follow the manufacturer's instructions.

3. Start at the ceiling, aligning the paper with the plumb line you drew on the wall. Roughly two extra inches should flop against the ceiling, and two more inches should flop below the top of the baseboard.

4. Smooth the paper using a smoothing brush or a plastic smoother (which looks like a wide spatula without the handle). Remove wrinkles by pulling a section of the paper away from the wall until you reach the wrinkle. Smooth out the paper as you lay it back against the wall.

5. Smooth from the middle out, applying enough pressure to push out the bubbles but not pressing so hard that you stretch or tear the paper.

6. Now it is time to trim the edges. Using a wide putty knife, press the paper against the ceiling, baseboard, or corner and trim it

with a sharp razor blade. (The putty knife provides a straight edge to guide the blade.)

7. Continue with the next piece, aligning it with the one you just laid down.

8. Roll each seam with a seam roller, but do not press so hard that you squeeze out the entire adhesive. Go back 10 or 15 minutes later and roll each seam again.

9. When you reach the end the place where you started you will want to create a clean final seam. Lap the final strip of paper over the first strip and trim both simultaneously.

10. Be sure to wipe any excess adhesive off the paper, ceiling, baseboards, and adjoining strips. Use a wet sponge, followed by a dry rag.

Painting is important when selling a home because it can create a huge change with just a little money and elbow grease. After you have taken care of the walls, it is time to evaluate the kitchen and bath.

Making Those High Sale Rooms Pop

For most people, a complete renovation of a kitchen or bath is not possible, both in terms of time and money, yet both of these rooms are important. That is why most professionals would suggest that you update and refresh your kitchen and bath. You can replace a countertop, repaint the cupboards, add new door pulls, and even add some newer lighting without spending a lot of money.

Professional Bonus Tip: The kitchen and baths need to be model perfect because the kitchen and baths sell the home.

Having someone tell you to refresh your kitchen and knowing what that means are two different things. Here are some ideas to make your kitchen more desirable without a complete renovation.

1. Islands are a big amenity in a kitchen. You can create one by connecting a couple of stock base cabinets and adding a new countertop.

2. You can add flair to your cabinets by nailing crown molding where the ceiling and the cabinets meet to draw attention upwards and give your cabinets a lift without ever touching them.

3. Replace your cabinet hardware. You would be surprised at the difference it can make to a kitchen or a bathroom. At your local hardware store you will find a wide array of drawer pull designs from painted ceramic to metal knobs. Simply unscrew your existing cupboard hardware, replace with the new, and presto, you have completed a quick update for your home.

4. Put a new backsplash behind your sink in the kitchen and/or bath. You can use glass mosaics, porcelain tile, natural slate, or a faux paint finish for a unique backsplash.

5. If your sink is dingy-looking, you should considering replacing it. A stainless steel sink in the kitchen is always a good choice. A white sink is always a good choice for the bath.

6. Do you still have harvest gold or avocado green appliances from the '70s? They have to go. This is especially true if the market is slow. Buyers are going to choose a house with new appliances over yours, given two comparable homes. And they are likely to choose a house with newer appliances, even if your home has more amenities.

7. Add new window dressings that add a bit of spark to the room but do not obstruct the light.

PROFESSIONAL BONUS TIP:

Use faux painting techniques to paint your counters! You can paint them to look like granite and then add several coats of varnish. People will be amazed that it is not real granite!

Before you consider making any changes to your kitchen or bath, it is best to consider the market. Remember, the costs of renovation are only truly recouped when you consider marketability. If it is a sellers' market, you may not have to consider making a full renovation. If it is a buyers' market, you will have to do as much as possible to make your house stand out from others, including overhauling your kitchen.

Here are some simple techniques that can give your kitchen and bath a lift so that buyers take a second look.

Painting kitchen or bathroom cabinets

Replacing kitchen cabinets can be costly, but so can trying to sell a home with a tired-looking kitchen. If your cabinets are sturdy and in good condition other than looking drab, you may want to consider painting them. Here is how:

1. Remove all the hardware from the doors and drawers. This includes the handles, pulls, and hinges.
2. If the drawer fronts can be removed, do so. Pull out the drawers and set aside.
3. Clean all surfaces with a mixture of water and trisodium phosphate (TSP) and a sponge or an abrasive pad.
4. Wipe all the surfaces dry.
5. Look for dents or scratches. Repair them with spackling compound applied with a putty knife.
6. Let the spackling dry thoroughly.
7. Check any new hardware to see if they fit the existing holes. If not, fill in the old holes with spackling compound.
8. Sand the surfaces to be painted with coarse sandpaper so the paint will adhere more completely.
9. Make certain you sand all the nooks, crannies, and rounded edges.

10. Paint the backs of the doors first. Let dry and then paint the front faces, including drawer fronts. You can paint the doors with a standard-sized paint roller. Paint the edges with a brush.
11. Use a little paint roller for the face frames.
12. Let everything dry completely before you begin to reassemble.
13. Screw the hinges to the doors and then back to the face frames.
14. Reattach all the handles and the pulls or add the new ones.
15. Apply rubber or felt bumpers on the backs of the doors to prevent the paint from sticking.

Although repainting your cabinets can save a lot of money, it makes no sense to do so if your cabinets are falling to pieces. Trying to make something shabby appear new with a bit of paint will make your buyers feel as though you are trying to hide problems. If you are willing to hide something like poor cabinets, what else could you be hiding? If your cabinets are in poor shape, your money and time will be better spent buying and installing new ones.

How to replace a faucet

You will need to replace the faucet if it is broken or if it no longer looks new. Rather than hiring a plumber, here is how you can do it yourself.

Remove the old faucet

Step 1: Shut off the water. You can turn off the main water valve, or turn off the two valves immediately under the faucet you are replacing. Then open the faucet and allow it to drain and release any pressure.

Step 2: Disconnect the water supply lines. If you choose not to replace the lines, disconnect them from the faucet only. If you choose to replace them, disconnect the lines from the shutoff valve.

Step 3: Remove the faucet from the sink. Bottom mount faucets are removed from above, and the handles and escutcheons must be removed to get to the nuts, which secure the faucet in place. Top mount faucets are held in place by nuts located under the sink, and they must be removed from below. The nuts may be loosened using water pump pliers or a special basin wrench, available at Home Depot or Loews. The basin wrench is necessary when the area in which the nut is located is too tight to allow the use of pliers.

Install a new top-mounted faucet

Step 1: Apply a bead of plumber's putty or silicon caulk around the perimeter of the faucet base. Faucets that have rubber or plastic gaskets for the base do not require this step.

Step 2: Ease the faucet into place, pressing against the putty to make a good seal.

Step 3: Under the sink, install the washers and mounting nuts on the tailpieces, tightening the nuts by hand.

Step 4: Align the faucet with the back of the sink and tighten the mounting nuts with water pump pliers, an adjustable wrench, or a basin wrench. Wipe away excess putty or caulk from around the base.

Install a new bottom-mounted faucet

Step 1: Hold the faucet in place from under the sink.

Step 2: Install the washers and mounting nuts, tightening the nuts by hand. Align the faucet with the back of the sink and tighten the mounting nuts with water pump pliers or a wrench.

Step 3: Run a bead of plumber's putty along the base of the escutcheons and screw them in place.

Step 4: Install the faucet handles. The one marked hot should go on the left. Wipe away excess putty from around the base of the escutcheons.

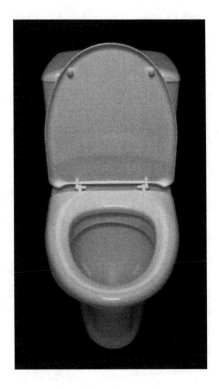

Replacing the toilet

Toilets only need to be replaced if they are cracked or happen to be harvest gold, avocado green, or some other out-of-date color. Although not a tough job, replacement can be messy.

Most home improvement tools and materials are available at Home Depot or Loews. To replace the toilet, you will need the following tools:

- Adjustable crescent wrench
- Putty knife

You will also need the following materials:

- New toilet
- Wax seal ring
- Rags
- Plastic grocery bags
- Wet vacuum cleaner

Before you begin, shut off the water by turning the valve behind the toilet. Then flush the toilet to remove as much water as possible from the tank and bowl.

First you will need to remove the old toilet. Use the crescent wrench to loosen the bolt attaching the hose to the water valve and remove the hose. Next, use the wet-vac to remove the remaining water from the tank and bowl of the old toilet. Remove the bolt covers from the base of the toilet and use the wrench to remove the nuts from the bolts attaching the toilet to the floor.

Once the nuts are removed, you can now lift the old toilet out of place.

Now that the old toilet is removed, take the rags and stuff them into the plastic grocery bags. Then take the bag and put it firmly inside the drain to keep any sewer gases from coming up from the drain into your bathroom where you are working. The great thing about using plastic grocery bags and rags is that when you are done with the next step, you can remove the bags by their handles and keep your hands from getting dirty.

After the drain is stopped up, take a putty knife and scrape away the remnants of the old wax seal on the floor where the old toilet sat.

Now it is time to install the new toilet. It is easy if you follow these directions:

1. First, take the plastic bag out of the drain.
2. Take the wax seal ring, which looks like a doughnut, and place it over the drain.
3. Lift the toilet into place over the floor bolts and place it on top of the wax seal.
4. The weight of the toilet will flatten the wax ring and give your toilet a good seal.
5. Then reattach the nuts to the floor bolts to hold the toilet firmly in place.
6. Using the crescent wrench, reattach the water line to the valve on the wall behind the toilet.

Simply turn on the water, flush the toilet, and you have upgraded your bathroom in about an hour.

Laying bathroom or kitchen tile

Do you think that updating the bathroom or kitchen with some new tile will do the trick? Then just follow these steps to do it yourself.

You will need the following tools:

- Hammer
- Pry bar
- Carton knife
- Cutoff saw
- Wet saw or tile snips
- Grout saw
- Mixing bucket
- Notched trowel
- Sponges
- Shop Vac
- Rubber trowel
- Drill with mix bit

You will also need the following materials:

- Tiles
- Thin set
- Grout
- Chalk line

Start by removing the carpet and carpet strips or the old vinyl flooring. Use a cutoff saw to make room for the tile to slip under the doorjambs. Place a portion of the tile pattern starting at the doorway to establish a centerline and then strike a chalk line accordingly.

Cut the tile with a wet saw or tile snips for smaller jobs as needed. Work your way up one side of the room and down the other. Allow 1/8 inch for grout lines; spacers can be used for uniformity.

Mix the thinset using an electric drill with a mixing bit. Mix small amounts at a time, adding water slowly to maintain the right consistency; you do not want it runny. Keep the drill at a slow speed to avoid creating air pockets in the thinset, and be ready to go to work because the thinset dries quickly. Mix enough to lay down a dozen or so tiles at once, using a notch trowel to apply the thinset to the floor.

When the tile is all in place and somewhat dry, use a grout saw to scrape the excess thinset out of the joints where the grout will go. A shop vac will clean most of this up, but use a wet sponge to get the surface clean.

When the surface is dry, begin applying the grout with a rubber trowel. Grout is available in a variety of colors and mixes easily with water. Again, mix slowly to avoid too wet a mix. Just slop it on the tile surface working it into the grout lines and do not worry about the excess grout, as it will clean up easily with a sponge as long as its still wet, so do small areas at a time. One more sponge cleaning will be required to get up the film once it is completely dried.

It is recommended to apply a grout sealer after about 48 hours to help avoid stains that would occur during normal use.

PROFESSIONAL BONUS TIP:

Consider reglazing your tub. For about $35, you can reglaze a tub and the surround. Just follow the directions. You will not believe the difference it can make.

Laying vinyl tile

Vinyl tile is a simple, inexpensive way to cover a floor. Many tiles have a self-adhesive that only requires peeling off the backing and sticking them down. Tiles without the backing require spreading an adhesive over the floor with a notched trowel and then setting the tiles.

1. Determine the number of tiles you need for the size of your room. For twelve-inch tiles, it is a simple calculation. Just multiply the length by the width of your room (area) – that is the number of tiles needed. Add 5 percent extra for cutting and waste. Nine-inch

tiles require dividing the room's length (in inches) by nine, then dividing the room's width (in inches) by nine. Take those two numbers and multiply them together to get the number of tiles needed. Again, add 5 percent extra. All the major obstructions on the floor like cabinets and appliances should be measured separately and subtracted from the total.

2. Next you will need to prepare the subfloor and underlayment. Vinyl tends to mirror any irregularities in the floor that it covers. All joints and holes in the underlayment should be filled with floor patching compound and sanded to make a smooth surface.

3. Check that there is adequate clearance at the bottom of doors to allow for the new floor.

4. Remove baseboard before installing the floor.

5. Read over and follow the adhesive directions to ensure a proper bond.

To start laying the tile, you will need to divide the floor into four sections.

6. First, snap chalklines between center points of opposite walls. Check the intersection with a framing square to make sure the lines cross to form ninety-degree angles.

7. Lay tiles along the first quadrant guidelines all the way to the wall (alternating colors if you choose). If including a border, determine its width and snap a guideline around the floor's perimeter so the border tiles will look uniform.

8. Lay tiles square with the lines, working diagonally across each quadrant. Starting from the center point and working back toward the walls, lay the tiles in horizontal rows.

9. Check that the tiles lay out correctly; then gather them up. Peel the backing off and press tiles into position, checking that they are square with the guidelines or their neighboring tiles. Or spread glue over a manageable area and lay each tile into position. Keep some clean rags on hand and wipe up any excess glue.

10. Repeat the process for the other three quadrants.

Tiles rarely fit exactly the length or width of a room. Tiles in the last row usually need to be trimmed to fit.

11. Lay a loose full tile (this is the tile we will cut) directly on top of the last installed full tile in the row. Line up the edges and pattern lines.

12. Set another loose full tile to act as a template on top of the first loose tile and slide it tight against the wall over the space that needs to be filled in. Make sure it lines up straight with the row. A portion of the bottom tile will be exposed past the template's edge that is the piece you need.

13. Use the edge as a guide and mark a pencil line on the first tile.

14. Remove the template tile and cut the marked portion off the full tile. Test-fit the piece to make sure it fits well. Then glue and press it in place.

15. After all the tiles are laid, roll out any air bubbles or extra glue. For large rooms, a 100-lb. roller (rental item) will save a great deal of time over hand rolling, but a rolling pin works fine for small areas.

You do not have to stop with the kitchen and the bath. There are many other areas of the house that can be repaired or refreshed.

Stop Them in Their Tracks

Whether you have an expensive home with a grand foyer or a more modest home with a small square of entrance space, you will definitely want to refresh the look. This is the first thing a buyer will see upon entering your home. If your entrance way feels fancy and rich, the buyer will feel that your home is fancy and rich. This feeling will follow them throughout the home tour. When the offers come in, they will reflect this feeling.

The reverse is also true. If you have a shabby entryway, your buyer will feel that your entire home is shabby simply because their viewpoint has been colored by their first impression. Feelings of shabbiness do not lead to high offers.

One of the best ways to create a rich environment in the entryway is to change the flooring. If your house has wood or carpeted floors, making your entryway floor a different material will help to set it off from the rest of the house and define the space. One of the best ways to do this is to add tile.

Tile has been used in homes for centuries. It was the material used in villas and palaces back in the days of Ancient Greece and Rome. The richness experienced then is still experienced today.

If you do not want to use tile, you can consider hardwood to offset carpet or a synthetic material. Synthetic materials can look like granite, cobblestone, or tile. The point is to make your entryway grand.

When a guest walks into your entryway, are you proud of what they see? If not, then you need to make changes.

Watch It Open, Watch It Close

Windows and doors often require attention. Do your windows open easily? Do your doors squeak? Something as simple as a stuck window can cause an uneasy feeling in the mind of a potential buyer.

Check all of your windows to make sure they open and close easily. Summer heat and humidity swell the wood, causing sudden friction between the window and the window trim.

Luckily, it is an easy fix: Carefully pry the trim off, then spray a lubricant such as furniture wax or WD-40 along all the surfaces where trim and window meet. Finally, nail the trim back on.

Now take a look at the windowpanes. Do you have any that are cracked or broken? If so, replace them before you begin showing your home.

Before starting to replace broken glass, put on a pair of gloves and a pair of glasses. It is easy for bits of glass to chip and fly. Glass, in both wood and metal frames, is normally held in place by a mechanical fastener. In wood they are usually glaziers' points, small triangles of thin metal. In metal window frames, spring clips are used. Putty or glazing compound is then applied to keep out rain.

The following steps are suggested for replacing broken window glass:

1. Carefully remove all pieces of glass in the area around the window to prevent injury and cuts. Use pliers to grip pieces of glass still in the window.
2. With a chisel or jackknife, remove the old putty. Be careful not to gouge the wood frame. As you proceed around the frame you will find glaziers points (small steel triangles) in wood frames or spring clips in metal window frames. Save the points or clips. Be sure all old putty is removed so the glass will slide into place easily.
3. With sandpaper or a rasp, clean off bits of putty that remain on the wood or metal sash.
4. Paint the frame with an oil based wood preservative or an oil base primer. This seals the wood surface under the putty and prevents the metal frame from rusting. A fast-drying primer is the most convenient.

5. Measure the size of the glass with a yardstick or folding rule. A steel rule may sag causing errors in dimensions. Allow 1/8 inch clearance on all sides so reduce each measured dimension by 1/4 inch. Buy the glass cut to the correct size.

6. Put a thin ribbon of glazing compound in the groove on the frame for the glass to rest on. Keep the thickness of this glazing compound fairly uniform so that when you press the glass down into the compound it will not crack.

7. Install the glass, press it onto the glazing compound, and insert the glazier's points (small metal triangles) that you removed. Push these in with a large screwdriver. If you use a hammer, be careful not to break the glass. The points should be placed every six to eight inches. The spring clips for metal windows should be inserted in the holes provided in the steel frame.

8. Knead the glazing compound and form it into strings no bigger than a pencil. Lay a string of compound along one side at a time and force it onto the glass and wood frame with the tip of a putty knife. Smudges from the compound can be removed later with a cloth dipped in mineral spirits or turpentine.

9. After the glazing compound has dried, paint it to finish sealing the seams between the glass and the compound, and the wood and the compound.

Now it is time to check your doors. Make sure they open and close properly without creaking. If they creak, a shot of WD-40 on the hinges usually makes the creak go away.

Also be sure the doorknobs turn easily and that they are cleaned and polished to look sharp. As buyers go from room to room, someone opens each door and you want them to have a positive impression.

Gray Cement or Grand Floor?

One final job you can do applies only if you have a basement or other room with a concrete floor. Concrete floors can look unfinished. In a buyer's eyes, unfinished floors mean unfinished space – space that is of no use.

Painting a concrete floor can make an incredible difference in the way a room looks and feels. Instead of unused space, you can create a useful area. Since basements are not usually pretty, having a way to increase the beauty without adding a lot of expense can make a big difference when it comes to first impressions.

This Could Be You:
A Real Estate Agent Success Story

The home's basement would not count as square footage in this city, so it was not listed. However, I knew that it could be a big bonus when buyers saw it. The basement was almost finished with concrete walls, a drop ceiling, linoleum flooring, and some shelves that were not painted.

I had the owners paint the walls and the shelves the same color. I also had them put in a few pieces of furniture — a loveseat, a chair, and a table with a lamp plus a few greeneries.

Immediately, people saw this as a family room instead of an unfinished basement. They got far more money for the house because even though the square footage did not count on paper, it did count in their minds. All it took was a little bit of paint and a little bit of time.

Basement Before

Basement After

This is a long project and cannot be finished in one weekend. Therefore, if you need to get your home on the market immediately, this job will have to go undone.

1. If your floor is inside the house, do a little checking before you decide to paint it. Is the concrete damp? If so, you may have to waterproof walls and floors, grade the yard so water falls away from the foundation, install a sump pump, or install drains around the foundation. This is especially important if you are thinking about installing a rug or some type of basement flooring. This can cost a lot of money, so understand the cost of flooring a basement. You must also be aware of The International Residential Code (IRC), which says a basement living space must have a clear, floor-to-ceiling height of at least 7 feet. However, if you just plan to paint the basement floor, and you find a leak or crack, fix it with an elastomeric sealant made specifically for concrete! Use a 3-foot or longer bubble level to see if any sections of the floor slope more than a half-inch in 8 feet. Fill in low spots with a self-leveling compound, available at home improvement centers for about $30 for a 50-pound bag. For about $60 to $80 per day, rent a concrete sander to reduce high spots. If you are just painting concrete, you will have to wait for the concrete to dry out, probably several days. If this is the case, you may want to forgo painting, but your buyers will be happy that the basement no longer leaks!

2. Thoroughly clean the concrete. If there is any grease on the floor, you must remove it because paint does not stick to oil. To remove grease, put down cat litter to absorb the majority of oil and scrub again with Goof Off. Then mix up a bucket of trisodium phosphate (TSP) and scrub the floor, rinsing several times, until your mop is clean. Wait at least three days for the floor to dry. You can stop here if you do not think that painting is for you.

At this point, you no longer have a leaking basement or a dirty concrete floor!

3. Sand off any paint, glue, or paint residue with a hand sander and 80-grit sandpaper. Vacuum well. Go over the floor with a tack cloth (a sticky cheesecloth available at any hardware or home improvement store).

4. Use elastomeric sealant specifically for concrete to repair any cracks and holes; let it dry completely. A 10-ounce tube runs from about $4 to $10 at home improvement centers.

5. Now we begin the painting process. Roll on two coats of Kilz primer and stain blocker. Let dry between coats.

6. Use a roller or a paint compressor, if you have one, to paint on at least two coats of a good latex flat paint. Let dry completely!

7. Roll on two coats of Breakthrough sealer with a 1/4-inch nap roller. You will need a respirator mask for this. Let dry.

Now you have a beautiful concrete floor – indestructible and colorful.

☝ PROFESSIONAL BONUS TIP:

Your major competition comes from newer homes. People will take a newer home over an older home if all else is equal. That is why it is essential to give an older home something that puts it above the rest.

CASE STUDY

What are the most important repairs to make on a home? I firmly that you need to focus on the outside! Look at your shutters, sidewalk, exterior paint, and windows. What do you see? Repair the cracks, hang the shutters correctly, pressure wash the sidewalks and driveways, and paint the exterior of the home. These simple things will make a world of difference. You only have a few minutes to make a good first impression, and the outside of the home is the first thing buyers will see. If your home is nice from the outside, it will draw them to the inside. This is known as "curb appeal."

That is not to say, however, that there is no need to make inside repairs. Paint is inexpensive and gives you a big bang for your buck. Although a bit labor-intensive, painting is not expensive and gives your home a new, fresh, clean look.

Then look around your home carefully. What do you see? If windows are broken, they need to be fixed. Also look at the minor things. Fill in holes and finish projects such as trim and grout. Anything you can do to make your home appear "like new" will help your home sell.

I believe in helping a seller get the most money for their home using what they have. However, when it is warranted, I do suggest new carpet or a new sink. This typically happens if real estate agents or buyers leave with a bad impression concerning specific items in the house.

After you have repaired your home, it is time to look at the staging aspect. Any home can benefit from staging, whether it is a home that is over-decorated, over-crowded, or has poor furniture placement. All homes need to depersonalize. And all homes need to have some design for a warm, fuzzy feeling. The point is that you are working to appeal to more buyers.

Many people assume that staging costs too much money. This is simply not true. You would be amazed at the things a stager can use that you already have. Spending just a little can make a huge difference.

Other sellers have trouble separating themselves from their home. Sellers must realize that living is not the same as selling. Just take a look at the time, effort, and money builders invest to create model homes to help sell homes in a new community. They understand that the homes, although they cannot appeal to everyone, need to appeal to as many people as possible. After you put your home on the market, it is an item to be sold. When a stager asks you to take down an item or change your décor, follow the advice to sell your home quickly and for the most money. It is not a personal thing.

Whether you have a modest home or an expensive one, you can use staging to your benefit. The same general ideas apply to all housing. Despite the fact that many sellers believe that staging is for the higher end homes, the truth is that modest homes may need something that gives them a punch that a buyer would not expect – something with a bit of drama that creates interest or a buzz. I have even seen expensive homes that need some spice.

If you are in a modest home, do at least one thing that gives your home that upbeat feel. Go to the Salvation Army and get a particular piece of furniture to accent a feature in your home. Create inexpensive but dramatic window treatments. Put containers out front with colorful or unusual plants. You might need nothing more than a spectacular furniture arrangement. What you want to do is create something that makes the buyer remember your house.

The same is true of empty homes. Empty homes do not sell well because there is no drama. In fact, in empty homes, there is nothing at all. The only thing a buyer will remember is how empty the house was and how small the rooms seemed. This is not the impression you want to leave with a potential buyer. That means that you need to create some pizzazz by creating small vignettes, especially in the kitchen, family room, and front door. Also add some window treatments.

Repairing and refreshing are often all that is needed to make your home ready to sell. There are times, however, when a full remodel is needed.

Painting TIPS

13. Paint those walls! Within a day or two you can transform a room with color!

14. For a harmonious look, add a few drops of wall color paint to the white paint for the ceiling. Subtle, but effective!

15. Green or blue in the bedrooms are great colors because they are restful.

16. With a small nail, hammer small holes in the rim of a paint can. This allows the paint to drip back into the can and prevent the paint from dripping over the side of the can.

17. Paint during the day to get maximum lighting in the room, or use an extension cord to bring in a light source from another room.

18. Good quality paints require fewer coats and are easier to apply.

19. Flat paint is difficult to clean. Therefore, it is not recommended for high traffic areas. It is also not good for kitchens because you

will need to wash away kitchen messes, or bathrooms because any
steam will leave streaks. However, it does hide dents in the wall.

20. Matte finish and satin finish are good for special decorating
techniques. Since you are likely to be painting walls one color
and not decorating, you are not likely to need either matte or
satin finishes.

21. Semi-gloss is easier to clean and can be used for trims and walls of
high traffic areas.

22. Gloss finish is best to highlight trims and moldings and can be
used for windows and doors, too. It is easy to clean and you can
remove fingerprints from doors by quickly wiping them with a
wet rag.

23. When you are finished painting, organize the partially used
paints. Label them noting both the color and rooms in which the
paint was used. Buyers will be happy to have them on hand for
touch ups.

Wallpapering TIPS

24. A spatula, razor scraper or wallpaper steamer works as well as a wallpaper removers.

25. Corners and the areas behind opening doors are good places to start when beginning a wallpapering project.

26. Buy a roller (one you would use for painting) from your local hardware store and use it to saturate pre-pasted wallpaper. The roller spreads the water evenly and makes the job go quicker. I suggest using warm or hot water.

27. Most professional installers apply paste even to pre-pasted wallpapers, but be aware that this voids some manufacturers' warranties.

28. If a wallpaper pattern just will not line up between two strips, match it at the most obvious spot   eye level.

29. If you have an air bubble that just will not budge, poke it with a pin and press down on the paper before the adhesive dries.

Kitchen and Bath Repair TIPS

30. If you have dark cabinets, a light colored handle or something in shiny gold will enhance them. If you have light cabinets, you can give them the sleek look by using handles of the same color so that they are hardly noticeable or by using brushed silver handles. With light wood, you can also use darker handles, gold, bronze, or even colors.

31. A mirror with foggy spots around the edges or one with a painted frame makes the bathroom look old and dingy. Replace it with a new one. Be sure to have it large enough to fill the space but not so large as to overpower the room.

32. Wrap sandpaper around a sanding block for ease of use.

33. If you are removing an old sink and the nuts are rusted or corroded in place, apply penetrating oil and allow it to work into the threads before trying to remove the nuts.

34. When an old faucet has been removed, scum build-up may be on the sink where the faucet plate or escutcheons were attached. Clean it off with a 50-50 solution of vinegar and water. Scrape it away with a razor blade or scouring pad.

35. Before you remove the old toilet, take some newspapers and paper towels and put them on the floor. When you remove the old toilet, place it on the newspapers and paper towels to protect your floor or carpet from the dirt and old wax ring on the bottom of the old toilet.

36. When replacing bathroom floors, be sure that the flooring you choose is durable, water resistant, and not slippery when wet.

Window Repairing TIPS

37. When replacing trim on a window that has swollen shut, be sure to move it out 1/8 inch from its previous spot to compensate for that swelling.

38. Broken window glass can be replaced by regular glass or by plastic unbreakable glass, usually an acrylic.

Chapter 2

When to Remodel? That Is the Question

Sometimes a home or a part of a home simply needs to be overhauled. The most common remodel jobs include those in the kitchen (floors, cabinet refacing or replacing, counters, sinks, and appliances), those in the bath, converting an attic, finishing a basement, adding space, or changing a room's purpose (that is, from an office to a bedroom, or a bedroom to a study.) But how do you know when remodeling is worth it and when a simple paint job is all that you need? That is the million-dollar question!

You Can Recover Your Remodeling Costs – Sometimes

Determining if you are spending too much on a remodeling job comes down to recovering your costs. If you will not recover your cost when you remodel, it probably is not worth doing the project. Think about it, why would you remodel a room for $3,000 just to sell the house for the same price you would have without the remodel job?

Or even worse, what if you spend $3,000 remodeling your living room, only to find out for half that much money you could have updated your kitchen and sold your home for more.

According to Hanley-Wood LLC's 2014 Cost vs. Value Report, home owners recouped:

- 60 percent of the cost of an upscale bathroom addition when they sold their homes, and 60 percent of all kitchens on national average.
- 63 percent of the cost of an upscale kitchen renovation, and 74 percent of all kitchens on national average.
- 77 percent of the cost of a basement remodel on national average (including a main room, bar area, and bathroom).
- About 56 percent of an upscale master bedroom suite, and 67 percent of all basements on national average.
- 87 percent for a wood deck addition and 74 percent for a composite deck.

The stats of this report suggest that you should only renovate and remodel for your own enjoyment because these improvements will never fully pay for themselves. This is not entirely true, however. One thing the report does not take into account is how renovations affect the marketability of your home.

Real estate agents know that an up-to-date kitchen with new appliances, beautiful flooring, new counters, and spacious cupboards can sell a home on the spot. They also know, from far too much experience, that outdated harvest gold appliances, scuffed up linoleum, and cramped spaces can send buyers running as if a poisonous snake were in the kitchen.

The same holds true with bathrooms. If a house has two or more bathrooms with shining fixtures and nice looking sinks and toilets, a home will sell quite quickly far more quickly than a one-bath house with an avocado green sink, dingy fixtures, and tile with missing grout.

What this means for you is that if you have an outdated kitchen or bath or do not have enough baths in the house, you may be able to recoup the entire price of your updates by making it marketable. Earlier I mentioned the cost of staying in your home for four or five months. If you can save on the next mortgage and use that money toward the renovations, you really are not losing out at all, and if the renovations allow you to sell your house for more, you have really recouped your money.

Kitchen Remodels That Create Dramatic Effect

Spending $44,000 to get back only $33,000 does not seem to make too much sense. Unless you look further into the equation. A home with an outdated kitchen will either not sell or will sell for far less. Many real estate agents say that a fabulous kitchen will raise the price of a home $25,000 or more. Once that is added into the equation, the numbers seem to show that a kitchen remodel can truly be in your favor; that is, as long as your home warrants the updates.

Be sure that you are creating a kitchen that goes with your home. Adding top-of-the-line appliances and granite counter tops in a modest home is a mistake since there is no way to raise the sale price of the home enough to recoup the cost.

If you decide to remodel your kitchen, where should you start? There are five kitchen remodels that can create a dramatic effect.

1. Install new cabinets. What do you see when you first walk into the kitchen? The cabinets. They take up a large percentage of the visual space in the room and therefore they need to look good. They are also the most expensive part of any kitchen remodeling job.

2. Install new countertops. Next to cabinets, countertops are the next eye-catching feature of a kitchen.

3. Install new appliances   stove, oven, microwave, dishwasher, sink, garbage disposal, compactor, and refrigerator. This is imperative if the color or style of your appliances date the kitchen. Appliances more than ten years old often need to be replaced.

4. Install new flooring. There are many different types of kitchen flooring available ranging from wood to laminate to ceramic to vinyl. Be sure to match the flooring to the style of your home.

5. Install new lighting. At the least, you should have a light in the center of the kitchen and lights under the counters. Larger kitchens need lighting that allows you to make the most of the different workspaces.

If you decide to update your bathroom, you can follow the same pattern. However, instead of installing new cabinets, go for a new sink and faucet, and instead of new appliances, add a tub or shower.

CASE STUDY

Staging is really the process of making a house as inviting as possible to the most number of buyers. It is often difficult for purchasers to look beyond personal items or styles of decorating to see the house. In staging a property, my goal is to have the house appeal to the greatest number of purchasers. They should be able to imagine their belongings and furniture, rather than feeling that a home must be furnished or arranged in a certain way.

Many home owners balk at spending money on a property that they are preparing to leave. What they do not always understand is that an appealing home will generate more income than a "fixer-upper.

I also run into the 'it was good enough for me' attitude. If someone has been living with stained carpeting, they may not recognize how it looks to other people. This is the hardest objection to overcome. Just because a seller was willing to put up with a sub-standard property does not mean a buyer will.

After I get them to understand the need to make changes, I walk the house with the sellers several times and make sure that they have a good sense of what must be done to sell their property. Most are willing; they want to sell it for as much money as possible.

I have recommended bathroom renovations and minor kitchen renovations if the property is in a neighborhood where comparable homes have been renovated. In such a case, the home owners need to be prepared to bring their house up to market standards or accept less money than other properties have earned.

The price point of the home drives the amount required to get it up to market standards. The more expensive a property, the more expensive the renovations will need to be to "keep up with the Joneses." A house priced over $1 million will HAVE to have granite countertops if that is what the other houses have, or the seller can expect to make pricing concessions. A less expensive property may need new appliances (priced at the lower to mid-range) to compete with other properties in the same price range. All price points require well-maintained exteriors.

I suggest to everyone that they paint, both to neutralize the house and to improve the condition of the property, replace old or stained carpet, clean up the landscape and add plants, repair the front door and entrance area since first impressions are critical, and replace any exterior dry rot.

One of my home sellers in McLean, Virginia, had this to say about staging: "We were so pleased with the way in which our agent completely handled every detail involved in the sale of our Reston home. The way our agent packaged our home to get it ready for the sale, marketed our home, handled open houses, offers for sale and even the closing was professional, thorough, attentive, and caring. Our agent handled every aspect of this sale so completely that we were never overwhelmed or stressed. It made the sale of our home easier and more enjoyable than we could have imagined."

Remodeling Projects to Avoid

Buyers are far more concerned with living space. And they do not consider basements living space unless you happen to have a wonderful, fully finished recreation room. If you have a basement, it needs to be clean, but you do not have to renovate it to get a buyer.

The same goes for your yard. You will want it to be neat, but there is no need to add gardens, walkways, and rock walls. Nor is there a need to add a swimming pool or Jacuzzi. Although nice features, you will not recoup your cost.

Here are some other projects to avoid:

1. Adding high end appliances to a modest home
2. Adding hand painted tiles to the bath or kitchen
3. Adding a central vacuum
4. Adding air conditioning, unless you are in an area where all homes have it
5. Replacing windows with newer models

Beyond the Kitchen and the Bath

Stay simple with your remodeling and look at your home as though you were the buyer. Chances are that if you find a larger window could brighten the upstairs bedroom, potential buyers will probably feel the same.

Replacing worn carpeting, tiles, and wood floors can give your home an immediate advantage over similar properties in the area. It is recommended that you use neutral colors, such as gray, beige, and off-white when adding new floor coverings.

Do not go overboard. Concentrate on improving two or three deficiencies in your home. More than likely, the time and money you spend adding quality to your home will be rewarded with greater profit at selling time.

Remodeling TIPS

39. Be sure to check with your city or county building inspector before beginning a new project. Many departments require permits, even for things as simple as changing a dishwasher.

40. If you replace the kitchen sink with stainless steel, do not scrimp. Buy the high-end sink so that water will not create unsightly stains.

41. When buying a refrigerator, be sure to buy something you like you will probably take it with you.

42. Be sure to buy appliances that are the right size for your kitchen. Buying a large top stove that takes up too much space in your kitchen will not add value, but make the kitchen seem small.

43. Consider using granite only on the island and a less expensive covering for the rest of the countertops.

44. Here is a big no-no. Do not add a pool in hopes of getting a higher price on your home. Yes, the potential buyers will love it (unless they have small children) but they will not pay more to have it. Whatever you sink into a pool is going to stay there.

Chapter 3

Be a Clean Machine

It is a well-known fact: clean houses sell faster. *The Wall Street Journal* ran an article on this subject, recommending was to make sure that your home is absolutely clean. I concur whole-heartedly. Your home should sparkle! A dirty, untidy home tells buyers that they do not want to live here. A clean house brings about a feeling of peace and satisfaction. There is nothing quite as unsettling as a house that desperately needs attention.

PROFESSIONAL BONUS TIP:

If your house is not clean, no amount of staging can cover that up.

The good news is a clean home can be tips from the professionals. If you do not have time to invest in really cleaning your home yourself, it is worth hiring a professional cleaning company. This includes washing windows inside and out and cleaning blinds and screens. Buyers want to be able to see out!

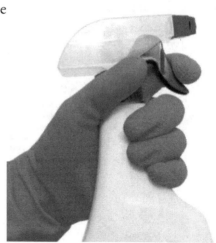

What Your Mother Tried to Teach You

Even before you clean, there are a few things you should take into consideration so that your cleaning can be done as painlessly as possible.

The first thing you need to do is wear comfortable old clothes that you will not mind staining or getting dirty. Once dressed properly, you need to take stock of your cleaning needs and supplies. Do not wait until you are about to clean the oven to find out that you do not have any oven cleaner left. Have everything on hand and ready to go for a smooth time.

REALITY CHECK

✓ Kittens are adorable, yes? What about their litter box? What about a litter box in the kitchen? The whole staging viewpoint is for the kitchen to be fresh and clean. The litter box was going to have to go! However, the seller would not put it in the basement because she felt that her cats should not have to go to the basement because basements were not for cats. The compromise was to put the box in the bathroom. It was at least where that kind of thing happens!

Everything in its place is a good motto to remember. Always find appropriate places to store your items. Litter boxes in the kitchen and trash cans in the pantry are just two examples of inappropriate placement.

Now, get the supplies ready to travel. Prepare one bucket of supplies to bring with you to every room. All you really need are a few rags, some paper towels, furniture polish, and one good all purpose glass and counter cleaner. These items will do the trick for most cleaning jobs. Also, grab two empty garbage bags: one to carry garbage you find along the way, and the other to fill with things you no longer want but are still useful. Any items in the second bag are those that you can give away or sell at a later date.

PROFESSIONAL BONUS TIP:

Do not have any cleaning products visible. You want the buyer to think that the house cleans itself. You do not want to remind buyers that there will be work to do in this house. Put away laundry baskets and dish drainers as well!

The best way to start is to clear it off and put it away. In the living room this means putting away books and recycling old magazines. Clear away all knickknacks and family photos so that dusting and polishing can be finished in a snap. In the bedrooms remove items stored under the bed and file away or throw out papers. In the kitchen remove everything from counters and take down curtains. In the bathroom clear away potpourri holders, magazines, and wastebaskets. Take down the shower curtain and liner for laundering. Remove these items and cleaning will be much easier.

PROFESSIONAL BONUS TIP:

Everybody in the family has to pitch in to move this property. And that includes keeping it clean.

Now that you have an understanding of cleaning basics, let's get down to the details!

CASE STUDY

Many people assume that staging is only for expensive homes or homes in big cities. However, this is not true. Inexpensive homes tend to be smaller, so they can often require more uncluttering. Since it is crucial to open up a small room to make it appear spacious, correct room arrangement is a key.

The best tip is really to "wow" the buyer when he or she walks in the door. The first few seconds upon entering the home are crucial. That is why staging can benefit all different types of dwellings   everyone needs the "Wow Factor."

Many people who are selling less expensive homes do not realize the value of cleaning, uncluttering, rearranging furniture to open up small spaces, and doing quick fixes that can increase the value of the home they are trying to sell. These same techniques are used in all homes, but can have a greater impact in small spaces.

The other thing that most home owners do not understand is that they need to put away personal items such as photographs and mementos. Potential buyers want to be able to envision their belongings in the home and have trouble doing so if you appear to be staying with the home. I am not suggesting that the home be cold and sterile. To the contrary, it needs to be warm and inviting, but it needs to invite them to move in and they can do this only if you allow them to do so visually.

When I stage, I use as much of the existing furnishings as I can. It often amazes buyers when they see the potential of their own items placed correctly. If there is a need for a couple of additional items, they can be rented or purchased. Usually the home owner is quite excited about getting a few new things because they will be able to use them in their new home.

Buying or renting furniture is especially vital in an empty home. Empty homes do not show well and can sit on the market for months until a buyer with a good visual imagination comes along or until the seller drops the price so low that the home is a steal.

When it comes to repairs, a fresh coat of paint can often be enough. Filling holes in the walls and replacing worn carpet will also make a big difference. The goal is to make your home look fresh and clean and to increase its value.

That is not to say that a seller should never do a remodel or a renovation. If there is something that can be changed that will really benefit the sellers and it is something they can afford, I would certainly suggest that it be done. However, large renovations do not always make sense because the seller is not going to get a good return on the investment. Adding a $40,000 kitchen will not increase the value of most homes by $40,000. Adding new countertops and refacing the kitchen cabinets for $400 will.

Following a few simple staging rules will increase the value of your home. Why would you choose not to do it?

So Clean You Can Eat Off the Floor

Although the entire house needs to be clean, there are two rooms where it is imperative: the kitchen and the bathroom. People serve food and eat in kitchens and they want them to be clean. That is why restaurant inspections are posted – people want to know how the restaurant fared on the cleanliness issue. If you show buyers a dirty kitchen, they will move on. They will assume that since your kitchen is not clean that you have not taken the time to care for any other part of the house.

The problem with saying "clean the kitchen" is that the instructions are not specific enough. I am sure your kitchen is just fine for living, but is it fine for selling? Do you know to give all your kitchen cabinets a good scrubbing? Do you know the best way to clean your appliances? Are you aware that even if your appliances are going with you that a potential buyer may walk away if they are not clean?

A really clean kitchen has had the following things done:

1. Cabinets and drawers have all been wiped down, inside and out. For glass or laminate, use a glass cleaner. For wood, use wood soap.
2. Small appliances have been wiped down. Even if you are storing them in a cupboard, you will want them to be spotless. Buyers will peak into your cabinets and if they see food stuck to your mixer, they will not be impressed.
3. The vents and hoods have been cleaned.

4. The sinks have been polished, including getting rid of all the grime that collects around the faucet!
5. The windows have been washed.
6. The walls have no greasy splatters.
7. The curtains are either new or have been washed so that they look and smell fresh.
8. The light fixtures have been emptied of bugs and even the light bulbs have been dusted.
9. The floor shines.
10. The woodwork gleams.
11. And do not forget the stove, oven, and refrigerator!

PROFESSIONAL BONUS TIP:

When a prospective buyer comes in, you want them to linger in your home. If things are clean, they envision their things and when they are envisioning, they are lingering. That is a good sign.

Cleaning the refrigerator

Your refrigerator will need to be cleaned, even if you are not leaving it. People will still look inside, and a dirty refrigerator will turn them off. If you are taking it with you, you may as well clean it now. If you are leaving it, then it is imperative to have it sparkling.

A frost-free refrigerator dehydrates its interior, turning liquid spills into caked-on lumps. To remove these "lumps" of food, soak removable parts in warm, slightly soapy water or a solution of one or two tablespoons of baking soda for every quart of warm water. Loosen a hardened spill on fixed parts by covering it with a damp sponge or cloth; use a toothbrush in crevices. Do not use bleach or ammonia, which can damage some surfaces.

Other than spills, refrigerators tend to have odors. Why? Because the plastic linings absorb odors. Before tackling them, move food to a cooler or into paper bags wrapped in an old quilt or blanket for insulation. Unplug the refrigerator, wash the interior with the baking-soda solution mentioned above, and wipe it dry. When the refrigerator is on again, slide a shallow pan of activated charcoal (available at plant nurseries and pet stores) onto a shelf. If odors return, recharge the charcoal in an oven at 300° for an hour and try again.

Another way to get rid of odors is to place an open box of baking soda inside the refrigerator to trap the smells. When you notice the odor, replace the box with a fresh one.

If the bad smell is still there after two weeks, place a small dish of vanilla extract in the refrigerator to mask it. Do not use odor-control products with a lemon scent because the fragrance sinks into plastic and stays there.

 PROFESSIONAL BONUS TIP:

Always do the sniff test. If you can smell it, so can the buyers!

And finally, it is time to look at the coils. Refrigerators cool by stripping heat from the air inside the compartment and releasing it through condenser coils. Dust acts like insulation on the coils and keeps them from releasing heat efficiently. Clean the coils with a vacuum wand or a long-handled brush.

Older refrigerators may have coils located in the back. To avoid damaging your floor, try to clean them without moving the appliance. In newer ones, the coils are usually at the bottom, accessible by removing the front grill. Although some models have coils that their manufacturers say never need cleaning, pet dander disproves that claim. Check coils periodically if you have cats or dogs.

Cleaning the freezer

Once the refrigerator is clean, it is time to tackle the freezer. You can clean a freezer and reduce odors the same way you did in the refrigerator.

Then there is the problem of ice build-up. In side-by-side refrigerator-freezers, ice can build up on the bottom and block the defrost drain tube. If you can see the drain hole, mix one teaspoon baking soda in two cups hot water; put it in a turkey baster, and squirt it into the hole. If this does not work or if you cannot find the drain hole (in some models, it is inaccessible), arrange for a service visit.

With old refrigerator-freezers, never try to pry ice off with a spatula or other tool; it might puncture the lining. Instead, turn off or unplug the appliance and store food as suggested above for cleaning a refrigerator. Melt ice with a fan or a hair dryer set on low.

Tired of being cold? Great. It is time to work on the oven.

Cleaning the oven

When you plan to sell your home, your oven needs to shine, so it is time for a heavy-duty cleaning. Wash racks by hand unless the owner's manual says they are dishwasher-safe.

Then try this homemade cleanser from "Clean House, Clean Planet," by Karen Logan (Pocket Books; 1997) for the baked on grime on the inside. Use aluminum foil to plug holes leading to the broiler. (Be sure to remove the foil after cleaning.) Mix 1/4-cup salt, 3/4-cup baking soda, and 1/4 cup water into a paste. Brush on, avoiding bare parts—salt corrodes metal. Let it sit overnight; remove mixture using a slotless spatula or a putty knife. Wipe with paper towels. Use a plastic scrubber or sponge to remove remaining spots.

Once the inside of the oven is clean, it is time to work on the stovetop itself. How you clean depends upon what type of stove you have.

Cleaning the stove top

There are three main types of stoves: **electric burners** (such as electric coil cooktops, modular cooktops, and induction stoves), **glass cooktops** (called electric ceramic smoothtops), and **gas burners** (which include modular cooktops and induction cooktops if used with a conversion kit). Here are the best methods for cleaning each.

Electric burners: Wipe food off burners when they are cold. If residue remains, open windows or switch on an exhaust fan, turn burners to high, and let the food smoke off. If plastic has melted onto a burner, scrape it off with a wooden spoon while coils are warm. Be sure to do this early enough in the selling process that your home does not smell like smoke when buyers arrive. If you have a showing in the near future, it would be best to buy new burners. The smell of burnt food will be far more costly than the price of a few burners.

Gas burners: You can wash porcelain-coated stovetop pans and grates by hand unless their manufacturer recommends putting them in a dishwasher. Dishwasher detergent is more alkaline than hand-dishwashing liquid, and the machines keep their contents damp longer. Both factors may cause rust at gaps in chrome or porcelain coatings. You may not see the gaps, but the dishwasher will find them. Uncoated metal parts are best soaked and then rubbed with a scouring pad.

Glass cook tops: If you have a glass cook top, then you know that these must be protected from scratching. Clean with a pad safe for nonstick coatings, and dedicate it to this use only. Wipe up sugary spills while they are still warm. For burned-on food, use a razor blade fitted into a plastic handle. Hold it at an angle of about 30 degrees, and carefully scrape with the full width of the blade, not just a corner. Follow up with a dab of commercial cook top cleaner on a dry paper towel; then wipe off the cleaner with another dry towel.

Now, it is time to move on to the next most important room of the house – the bathroom.

More Than a Swish and a Swipe

It is particularly important for bathrooms to be hospital-clean from top to bottom before the first showing. Scrub everything   shower walls, floors,

and countertops. Wash the shower curtains according to instruction and do not forget the bath mat. Even replace your plastic liner with a fresh new one! Although you want to make sure you use a good disinfectant, you do not want to make the bathroom smell like a hospital.

Having gleaming sink fixtures also makes a good impression. All your fixtures should look as good as new. If you cannot do this by cleaning, buy new ones.

This bathroom is clean and free
from counter clutter

PROFESSIONAL BONUS TIP:

Homes are not as clean as they could be. Bathrooms, drawers, and cabinets have to be immaculate like a hotel. Your drawers and cabinets get used and look used. Look at your drawers as if they were in a hotel. If you checked into a room with your current bathroom, would you stay? No one wants to buy your dirt!

They do not want to buy your dirt in the kitchen and bath, nor do they wish to buy it in your carpet or on your walls!

Let Them Look Down and Smile

Unless your carpet appears old and worn, or it is definitely an outdated style or color, you probably should do nothing more than hire a good carpet cleaner. However, if you want to tackle this yourself, it can be done. For best results, use professional cleaning supplies that suit your carpet type and fabric for general cleaning and stain removal.

You can also use a number of general household cleaning products to remove various substances that may get on your carpet.

1. Windex is helpful for removing paint.
2. For marker or pen marks you can use a cloth soaked in alcohol; dab – do not rub.
3. For liquid spills or pet urine first soak up the liquid with paper towels then clean the area with warm soapy water. Rinse with clean water and dry.
4. You can also use a combination of water and vinegar to blot the stain, remember to rinse and dry before sprinkling with baking soda or carpet deodorizer.
5. Shaving cream can be used as a spot stain remover for your carpets.

> ## PROFESSIONAL BONUS TIP:
>
> No one wants to buy your fleas! If you have dogs or cats that wiggle, squirm, and scratch, you have a flea problem! You may be able to live in your house this way, but you need to take care of it to sell! There are many products available for the carpet and upholstery to help you with this problem.

Stains and Crayons – On the Way Out

We all love the Van Gogh renditions that our children do on the walls; too bad they cannot do them on paper. As much as we would like to keep them, they must go – no, not the children, their little murals. Spray WD-40, wipe off immediately and bye-bye to the crayon marks. If the little tykes used permanent marker on any non-absorbent surface, moisten a cotton ball with regular rubbing alcohol, rub it on the surface, and off it goes.

Furniture that is stained can either be cleaned professionally, or with a rented cleaner, or it can be covered. Sometimes the best way to handle stained furniture is to remove it and put something else in its place. We will discuss ways of handling this in *Chapter 6: It is time to decorate.*

CASE STUDY

I recommend renovations only if absolutely necessary. Renovations slow down the time to get a house on the market. Painting is important, but there are lots of cosmetic fixes available, such as peel and stick floor and carpet tiles and paint for kitchen cabinets. Of course, there are those essential repairs that have to be done before the home goes on the market, such as fixing walls and ceilings, refinishing floors, and repairing roof damage.

In addition to having the repairs done, you must have your home clean and uncluttered before I arrive! This includes things like eliminating personal photographs and removing the contents of all closets by half. Both of these are often difficult for the seller to do.

In any home, I use props so buyers envision themselves "living" in the house. I want them to see themselves entertaining, relaxing, and reading with children. If I cannot fully stage each room, then I suggest minimal staging of "zones of influence," as well as any negative or questionable areas. Zones of influence include the entryway, living or family room, kitchen, powder room, master bedroom and bath. Believe it or not, one zone of influence can be the laundry room!

Each room should be embellished with accessories: artwork, mirrors, accent tables, silk trees and florals, as well as dishes, bedding, and towels so all areas look inviting. My goal is to give the buyer the ability to 'ponder the possibilities' for each space. With the exception of a fixer-upper, staging works wonders on all types of homes.

Let the Sun Shine In

Have you ever heard the phrase, "I do not do windows." If you are selling your house, that phrase needs to change to, "Where are the rags!" Clean windows mean more light and give any room a sparkle.

When it comes to window washing, there are some important tricks of the trade that you need to learn. Believe it or not, when you know what you are doing, you may actually find that you enjoy window washing.

The first trick is to arm yourself with the right window washing tools. This includes a good quality squeegee, applicator, scraper, window bucket, and microfiber cloths. The squeegee should be a 10-inch to 16-inch professional quality brass or stainless steel squeegee, depending on the size of window you will be cleaning. In addition to the squeegee, you are going to want a quality window scrubber and possibly an extension pole if you will be working on high windows.

Finally, you do not want to leave lint on the window from your cloths, so I suggest using microfiber cloths that are lint-free.

Your technique should be as follows:

1. Fill your window-washing bucket with cool or lukewarm water (never hot) and add a small amount of dishwashing soap.
2. Wipe away any cobwebs or debris on or around the window.
3. Dip the applicator into the bucket and run your hand across the applicator to get rid of excess liquid.
4. Wet the window with the applicator and scrub.
5. The window will begin to feel clean when it is done, as it will no longer have any rough patches. If you need to use a scraper to get rid of stubborn spots, be sure that the window is wet – never scrape a dry window.

Now, here are the tricks for a streak-free window. When window washing, you can ensure that you will not leave any streaks by using a dry rubber blade.

1. Place this blade against the top of the window, and pull down smoothly, using a rag to dry your blade between each stroke.
2. Repeat this process until the window is complete, being sure to overlap the

dry edge of the squeegee with the dry portion of the window to prevent drips and streaks.

3. To complete the window, you need to do one final stroke from left to right at the bottom of the window.

4. Use a dry microfiber cloth and run it around the edges of the window to soak up any remaining drips.

There is more to making the windows appear clean than just the windows themselves. If you have mini blinds or vertical blinds, they will need to be cleaned as well.

Mini blinds are convenient and attractive window treatments. The only disadvantage they have is that they cannot be cleaned easily. Cleaning mini blinds does not require strength – it just requires delicate handling. The following instructions should help.

As a first step, you should vacuum them to remove excess dust while they are still hanging on your window. Next, you should remove the mini blinds from the window and take them either outside or to the bathroom for a wet wash.

For the liquid washing component, you will need a hose, a clothesline, a bucket, and a sponge. Make a mixture of one-part water, to one-part ammonia in the bucket. Gently apply the mixture on the mini blinds, front and back. Allow the mixture to stand on the blinds for about five minutes, after which you just hose them. Wipe the mini blinds with a soft cloth and hang them on the clothesline to dry.

The above instructions are most relevant for cleaning cloth or plastic mini blinds. However, if your mini blinds are made of wood, clean them like you clean any of your wood furniture.

Vertical blinds are also important to clean. These simple vertical blind cleaning tips will help you keep on top of the cleaning.

Use a duster that will lift the dust right off the blinds rather than just move it around. After you have the major dust removed, take down the blinds. Depending on material, you may only need to vacuum the blinds. You can also soak, scrub, and rinse blinds to remove stains. Soak vertical blinds in the bathtub or rinse them outside with hose after cleaning.

Is That Fish?

Finally, we come to odors. Each home has a particular smell. The smell is a blend of cooking, people, and pets. As you are selling your home, you will want it to have a fresh clean smell.

PROFESSIONAL BONUS TIP:

Take a whiff of your house. We tend to overlook the unique smell of our own home. Those odors can be offensive. Get rid of food and pet odors. That is number one.

The problem is that it is difficult to smell the odors in your own home because you are used to them. The first time I drove into Pinehurst, North Carolina, I could not believe the incredible scent of pine trees. I felt as if I had entered Christmastime heaven. After just a few short weeks of living in the area, I never noticed them again. Did the smell go away? No – I just grew accustomed to my surroundings. The same happens in your home.

Reality Check

There was a home that had been on the market for a long time. The real estate agent finally brought in a stager. As the stager looked around and took notes, she found "it." "It" was a gerbil cage sitting on the coffee table in the living room. Gerbils are cute little pets, but no matter how adorable you may think they are, they are members of the rodent family, and when sellers see rodents, they think mice. And when they think mice, they think rat-infested home. And they move on. The gerbils had to go. In fact, they had to leave the house. In addition to creating the idea of infestation, they also had an odor!

Check for unusual odors in your house. It may come from a pet or even from your upholstery.

This is the time to get a fresh nose. Find someone you trust who will give you an honest opinion about your home's odors. What do they smell? Where do they smell it? Do not for one minute believe that smells will not matter. They will and they do! It is true that few sales rest on smell alone, but why leave a negative impression when you can do something about it.

For those who smoke, you might want to minimize smoking indoors while trying to sell your home. You could also purchase an ozone spray that helps to remove odors without simply masking the smell. As a current commercial says, "Nothing is worse than the smell of fish in your home   unless it is fish and flowers."

For those with pets, you will have some of the same problems as smokers. Pets have odors. You are probably used to them, but someone who walks into your house will notice them right away. This is especially true if your pet has urinated on the carpeting. The smell of pet urine can rarely be removed without replacing the carpeting. If you put your nose to the carpeting and smell your pet, even after shampooing the rugs, it is time to pull them out and replace them.

Keeping a home fresh smelling while living in it can be a chore. However, it is a chore that needs to be done.

Following these guidelines will make your home "white glove" clean. However, make sure you have cooperation from everyone in the family to keep their own personal spaces neat and clean. Remember, you never know when the right person is going to come along. Your house needs to be spotless always so that you can be ready for a home tour at a moment's notice.

PROFESSIONAL BONUS TIP:

Keeping your home in disarray will not appeal to the bulk of buyers. Yes, a small percentage will assume that they will get a good price if the house is in poor shape, but you want to appeal to a larger, higher-paying buyer pool.

Cleaning your home to sell it is an ongoing process to ensure that the home is in tip-top condition. When you are finished cleaning, it is time to go beyond clean and unclutter.

General Cleaning TIPS

45. Cleaning is rarely fun for anyone, but it does not have to be a terrible chore. Play some lively music. Before you know it, your adrenaline will start pumping and you will be dancing your way through the house.
46. Turn off the TV and the phone. The quickest cleaning is accomplished without any distractions.
47. Remember to tackle one room at a time.
48. Work around the room in one direction, either left or right. This way, there will not be any time wasted in criss-crossing the room, or vacuuming that same spot twice.

49. Wear rubber gloves. Even though it is harder to grip things with gloves than it is with bare hands, it is worth using them to protect your skin from the harshness of hot water and drying chemicals.

50. Ask a friend to help you assess your efforts – especially in sensitive areas such as odor removal.

51. Consider using a fresh citrus cleaner to get away from the institutional smell.

52. Use a good grout cleaner and a toothbrush on wall and floor tiles to make them sparkle.

53. Clean and sanitize wastepaper basket.

54. Make sure light fixtures, switches, switch plates, and outlet covers are clean.

55. You need to have your garage and basement immaculate and tidy. That sends a message. You want people to say that even the garage is neat or the basement is already to go. You want the impression that the house is ready to be moved into. This may be the biggest chore a person has.

56. Your ceiling is your fifth wall. Be sure to dust the cobwebs. This is even more important in texture sprayed ceilings – also known as popcorn ceilings – because dirt and cobwebs can get trapped in the bumps.

Cleaning Mixture TIPS

57. For cleaning glass shelves use a little white vinegar and water on a soft cloth. Wipe and clean. For metal shelves, use a little baking soda and warm water and wash with a soft cloth.

58. To clean those irritating stains in the bathtub, make a paste by using hydrogen peroxide and cream of tartar. Use an old toothbrush to rub into the stain and rinse thoroughly. No more having to open bathroom window, opening the door, and wearing rubber gloves.

59. Say goodbye to mildew with one word: bleach. Use lemon scented bleach and only 10 percent of it mixed with 90 percent of water in a spray bottle. Mildew is gone and you just saved an hour of using elbow grease. Do not forget to mark the bottle and keep out of children's reach.

60. Create a daily shower cleaner using the following recipe – 1 cup vinegar, 1/2 teaspoon liquid dishwashing soap, and 1/4 cup dishwasher rinse agent. You can also use a few drops of dishwashing liquid to a quart of water in a sprayer and a squeegee. Wipe with soft clean cloth. This cleaner leaves no streaks.

61. Clean dirty grout by spraying it down with Listerine. You will be amazed.

62. Baby wipes are miracle-workers on carpet stains, from motor oil to blood; they remove almost anything.

63. To remove pencil marks and other non-greasy spots from non-washable wallpapers, use an art-gum eraser or a slice of fresh rye bread.

64. To remove greasy spots, crayon marks, and food stains, apply a paste of cleaning fluid and fuller's earth, cornstarch, or whiting. Let dry and brush off. Repeat the treatment until the spot is gone.

65. To remove stickers and glue from furniture, glass, plastic, and other surfaces, saturate with vegetable oil and rub off.

66. To remove white heat marks and water rings on wooden furniture, try the following. If the wood has a good finish (do not try on bare wood), mix equal parts of baking soda and regular white, non-gel toothpaste. Lightly dampen corner of a clean, soft white cloth with water and dip into the paste. With circular motion gently buff the marks for a few minutes. Wipe area clean, and buff to a shine. Follow with furniture polish. (If rings remain after buffing five minutes or so, they may have penetrated the wood; you might have to refinish the piece). If that does not work, dip a cloth in vegetable oil, then in cigarette ashes, and then rub it over

the mark. Another method is to rub real mayonnaise onto the stain, allow to sit overnight, and then wipe with a dry towel.

67. Toothpaste will remove small scratches from glass.

Kitchen and Bath Cleaning TIPS

68. Scrubbing the cabinets with orange oil makes them look fresh, and also helps make the space smell cleaner, too.

69. Scrub your vent hood filter over your stove. Change the filter if applicable.

70. Fill a paper cup with water and a few tablespoons of baking soda. Nuke it for about 30 seconds, or until you see the contents explode. Then just take a paper towel and wipe it all off. The explosion spreads the cleanser over the entire area, and you can even use the moistened rag or paper towel to wipe outside the microwave and its surrounding area.

71. To avoid unpleasant odors in your refrigerator, store leftovers in covered containers or resealable plastic bags and wipe up spills promptly.

Vacuuming and Dusting TIPS

72. To prevent those nasty odors while vacuuming, sprinkle the rug with baking soda.

73. Spray your broom or dust mop with your favorite furniture polish, and the dust and dirt will be easier to collect when you sweep.

74. To dust papered walls, tie a dust cloth over your broom and work from the top down.

75. Wipe off fingerprints with a damp cloth and sprinkle the moist area with fuller's earth. Let it dry and then brush it off.

76. To prevent splash marks when you are washing baseboards or other woodwork, mask wallpaper with a wide ruler, Venetian blind-slat, or a piece of rigid plastic.

77. To pick up cat hair, put on a wet rubber dishwashing glove and wipe your hand over surfaces. The hair will stick right to it.

78. To help prevent dust buildup, rub down mini blinds with an anti-static dryer sheet.

79. Though window washing can be done at any time, the best conditions for washing windows are when it is a cool, cloudy (but not rainy) day. You never want to wash windows in direct sunlight because they will dry out too fast and leave streaks.

Odor and Noise Elimination TIPS

80. Home owners do not have an objective nose. You are used to living with your dogs, diapers, or cigarettes. Therefore, it is essential that you get an honest friend who does not come over all that often to tell you what it smells like. Houses that stink do not sell. Find out what makes your house have an odor and take care of it.

81. Do not undermine your efforts by reverting to smoking in your home. It is better to smoke outside while your home is on the market.

82. For those with cats, be sure to empty kitty litter boxes daily and use plenty of baking soda.

83. For dog owners, keep the dog outdoors as much as possible.

84. Try sprinkling carpet freshener or baking soda on the carpet on a periodic basis to keep down pet odors.

85. Do not use scented plug-ins or other overpowering deodorizing sprays. The strong smell of deodorizer will make buyers wonder what you are trying so hard to hide.

86. Noise can drive people away. Keep all radios off or playing low soft music and keep the windows closed if you have a lot of street noise.

This Could Be You: **TAKE A LOOK!**

This kitchen has no appliances on the countertops; it has just one simple accent piece to draw the eye further into the kitchen.

This tub says luxury and beckons buyers to imagine themselves soaking in the tub surrounded by glowing candles and soft music.

Chapter 4

Cut the Clutter

Defining Clutter

Really home staging is really about de-cluttering and making a home desirable to a much larger audience. Clutter keeps your home from selling quickly and for more money. Clutter is an equity eater. Even if you are an immaculate housekeeper, you are bound to have some clutter, especially if you view clutter my way.

There are many definitions of clutter. Some view it as junk. Some view it as stacks or piles. Some view clutter as messy tabletops or bookshelves. All of these are types of clutter, but do not really get to the heart of the matter.

Karen Kensington, in her book called *Clear the Clutter with Feng Shui*, explains clutter using four categories.

- Things no longer used or cherished
- Things that are not organized
- Too many things crowded into a small place
- Unfinished things

This definition gets to the heart of the matter. Due to the four broad categories, most people will find that they have clutter in at least one of these areas, if not more.

Take a look around you. Do you have items in your home that are unused and have no real sentimental value? These types of items can often be found in closets, cupboards, basements, and garages. Sometimes they are on bookshelves or even in your everyday living space.

What about items that are not organized? Do the books on the shelf look neat and orderly, or simply thrown into the space for books? Check on countertops and other surfaces. You are likely to find piles of bills, items to be filed, keys, and pencils. Check in your closet again. Is everything neat and tidy or do you fear opening the door because items are likely to fall out?

Now consider too many items in a small space. When I think of this, I envision my daughter's room. She loves to collect things and has everything: shells, porcelain dolls, horse figurines, and candles. Her room has a bed, desk, dresser, sewing table, end table, bookshelf, and each surface is covered in one of her many collections. This is fine for her. She is happy and loves to be in her room, but a buyer would find her room small even though it is an above average sized room. Why? There are too many things in the space!

Another example comes from a good friend's house. Her large family lived there for years. The house was relatively small and the den area always felt crowded. Just recently, they redecorated and put in two love seats in place of their old couch and loveseat, added much smaller end tables, and bought much smaller lamps. They also removed their bookshelf. You would not believe the difference. Of course, they were redecorating and not home staging, but the concept is the same. By ridding the room of so much extra furniture, it now feels large and spacious where it once felt small and crowded.

The final category is unfinished things. How many projects have you started that are not completed? These can be home projects such as painting the trim or they can be smaller things like a pile of clothes that need mending or an art project that is still waiting for the finishing touches.

Sherry Clark of Help-U-Out says, "I have never walked into an owner's home that is for sale and thought, 'Gee, if only they had more stuff!' The more you are able to move out the more the next buyer will want to 'move in.' However, if you actually do take up residence in your next home before your last one sells, you must move enough 'props' into your home so the buyer can understand the rooms' identifications. I have literally seen buyers hit their head on the dining room chandelier and wonder where to put the couch and television. Ninety percent of buyers cannot visualize what is not there!"

Do you want to know the best thing about uncluttering besides making more money on your home? If you really do it right and give away those unwanted items, packing to move and unpacking in your new home will get much easier. Before putting your home on the real estate market, figure out what you really need and what things you are just hanging onto for a rainy day.

PROFESSIONAL BONUS TIP:

Why stage to sell when you can stage to live! Get rid of stuff that you do not really need to live.

Four General Uncluttering Rules

Getting rid of clutter is one of the most challenging and beneficial actions for home staging. It is challenging because we all tend to hang on to our things – you never know, you may need it someday. When you hear those words in your head, eliminate them immediately – or the process of uncluttering will creep to a halt.

This Could Be You:
A Real Estate Agent Success Story

Staging works on all different types of homes. A granddaughter was given the task of selling her grandmother's mobile home. It was an older unit and the furniture was about the same age. However, there was no extra money to buy new furniture or even bedspreads or furniture covers.

It was a real challenge, but the agent worked with the furnishings and accessories at hand and sold the home quickly!

The older model mobile home after staging

To make this challenge more manageable, here are four rules to help you get started.

1. **Start with a plan:** If you go into a room with no plan at all, you are not likely to get rid of anything at all. One thing you might consider is how much you plan to eliminate. For instance, say to yourself, "I want to clear out 25 percent of this room."

2. **Make the time:** You will not be able to unclutter in 10 minutes. It is not possible unless you are only working on a limited space. If you have not made the time to do the job right, you will get distracted and probably give up. The other amazing thing that happens while you are away from the uncluttering process is that things that were partially uncluttered have morphed back to their original state. It is not until you have moved out those piles and created a more organized space that things will tend to stay that way!

3. **Know where everything you cleaned up is going.** This is a biggie. If you do not have a plan for what to do with the stuff you no longer need, it will get put in the basement, the attic, the garage, or stay in a pile. In that case, you just moved it to another location. When you are clearing the clutter for home staging purposes, you will have many different piles. Some things may go to a thrift store such as the Salvation Army, some things may go to the dump, some things may go into storage, and some things may be set aside for a garage or yard sale. Knowing what you are going to do with the extra clutter is essential to uncluttering your home.

4. **Remember why you are uncluttering in the first place:** You want to sell your house faster and for more money. Cutting the clutter is well worth the time and effort spent. Keep this in mind as the going gets tough or you start to waver and become overwhelmed.

Home buyers want to see a clean and clutter-free environment. The buyer wants the home to feel warm and inviting furnished their way. Unclutter your home, and they will get a good feeling about it.

Since it is easier to plan to do one room at a time rather than do the whole house at one time, the following sections of this chapter will give you hints and tips on how to unclutter each room or area.

Reality Check

✓ Can you imagine walking into a home and feeling like you were at an outdoor amusement park? Although it is a beautiful home, everywhere you look there is a carousel. Big ones, little ones, colorful ones. The collection was quite impressive, but it certainly was not going to help sell the house. The colors were bright and busy and no buyer could see past them to the wonderful features of the home. To make the house more salable, the collection of carousel horses was put into storage.

Do you have too much clutter in your home? Look at each room through the eyes of a buyer. Any clutter that you find should be thrown away, given away, or stored.

CASE STUDY

Home owners see their home through their own "lenses" and simply cannot see reality. They assume that whatever arrangement worked for them will work for other people, too, or that other people will not be bothered by the outdated décor or purple carpet they put in two years ago. Others are in denial about the overall condition of their house and argue about the necessity and costs of certain repairs and changes.

Then there are the home owners with pets who are negligent about the smells in their house, or people with smaller children who transformed their home into one big playground and think that is o.k. since everybody has children, right?

I always tell my home staging clients to step back and try to detach from their home as much as possible. Their house should be seen as the most expensive object they are ever going to sell. It needs to be presented in its best light to get top dollars.

Many people get nervous when stagers start changing floor plans, declutter their space and bring new items in, and ultimately force them to change their habits. This often evokes fear. They feel like it is not their home anymore and we tell them that is exactly how it should feel. Emotionally, it is not your house anymore when crowds of people start walking through, inspecting, judging, and bidding on it.

A home for sale should always be presented in its best light and immaculate condition, which is not the reality of everyday life. Potential buyers do not want to see how you live, with your children, cats, dogs, and messes. They want to see themselves in a perfect house under perfect conditions and that is how a home on the market should always be presented.

That means that sellers need to maintain a staged house in the same condition as I left it, which is a challenge for many people, especially families. Kitchens need to be clean all the time. Bathrooms should look like little spas, and no clothes, shoes, newspapers, or toys should be in sight. All beds must be made each day. And a good smell should flow throughout the house. This is a struggle for most sellers because even though they are selling, they are still living there!

Staging works on all types of homes. What I try to establish is a comfortable feeling and an attractive lifestyle that will please the majority of prospective buyers. The trick is to underline and enhance the positives and to take the attention away from the negatives. The goal is to provoke an emotional connection with the property: a warm feeling, positive memories, some excitement, and, ultimately, the desire to own it.

The materials that are used for staging should be in tune with existing materials in the house and also in tune with the architecture, age, and style of a property. I recommend materials that fit the house, which can be pricier in a more expensive home. I treat every house as an object that needs to be updated and embellished, no matter what the budget will be. In that sense, I do not treat inexpensive and expensive homes differently. Home buying is an emotional act and has a lot to do with psychology, past experiences, and desires, and it is my job as a stager to respond to that   no matter what type of property I am dealing with.

I often recommend renovations. A fresh coat of paint throughout a house has amazing results, especially when you choose the right colors for the right spots.

Everything should be in working condition so that there are no big repairs ahead for a buyer. Everybody likes a house in move-in condition and that is what it should always be. Surface materials like flooring or counter tops sometimes need to be replaced. Most prospective buyers do not want to take over an old, filthy carpet from the previous owners.

I also suggest quick bathroom or kitchen renovations if these rooms have an outdated feel and look versus the rest of the house. Nice kitchens and bathrooms are the biggest sellers, followed by good floors, and upgraded countertops. Home owners often remodel the kitchen, but not the bathrooms, or just the master bathroom and not the additional ones. By bringing all rooms to the same "level," the overall value of a house can be increased dramatically.

Every room in the house should be shown as what it is. For example, show a dining room as a dining room, even if the seller has been using it as an office. Buyers want to see formal living rooms, formal dining rooms, informal family rooms and functional kitchens and bathrooms. The master bedroom and bath should be shown as a special calm retreat where people can relax. By following these simple rules, your house can feel like a million bucks, or as a home owner in Hollywood Hills said, "My house was worth a million when I hired you. Now it looks like two million!"

Tackling Kitchen Chaos

Start the clutter-kicking in the kitchen since the kitchen is one of the most salable rooms in your house. Ask home buyers what area or room of the home they consider most important, and chances are they will say the kitchen. In fact, it has been said that people will buy a kitchen and the house that goes with it.

If that is true, having a great first impression in the kitchen is essential. When prospective buyers look at your kitchen, they will pay particular attention to its cleanliness, layout, and storage capacity. Clutter is not pretty and can add years to the look of a kitchen.

PROFESSIONAL BONUS TIP:

Most buyers are looking for openness. Therefore, you need to stage your kitchen and family room to make it appear as open as possible.

When prospective buyers come into your home, they will open everything – yes everything. They will open all your cabinets and drawers. They will look under your sink. They will peak in your pantry. If the appliances are staying, and sometimes even if they are not, they will check them, too. They want to be sure there is enough room for their "stuff."

PROFESSIONAL BONUS TIP:

Some people do not understand that people look in the cabinets. They NEED to see that those cabinets are adequate. It is not invading privacy.

If your kitchen cabinets, pantries, and drawers – even your refrigerator look jam-packed, you are sending a negative message to the buyer that there is not enough room in your kitchen. If they were looking for plenty of storage space, after opening your crowded cupboards they will believe your kitchen has none. The best way to change this negative first impression is to have as much "empty space" as possible.

Removing all the items on the counter will also give the impression of far more counter space. If you are not sure about the truthfulness of this statement, then take off the small appliances and set them into another room for a moment and take a look. You will be amazed at how much your kitchen grew in such a short space of time.

PROFESSIONAL BONUS TIP:

Take away everything on the kitchen counter. Does this mean the toaster? Yes, it does! It means the spices, too! Move it all. At most, have only one or two items on the countertop. People need to feel that the kitchen is big enough for their needs.

Do this kind of uncluttering with every cabinet and drawer. This will create a feeling of open space.

Another area that will need to feel open is the pantry. A pantry is often considered an amenity because it is an extension of your kitchen. But buyers will not find it to be an advantage if what they see is too much stuff and no organization.

Refrigerator before uncluttering

Keep in mind that a pantry is for storing food. It is not a good place for a dog's bowl, the cat's litter, or your garbage can. Even if you really use this space for those things, they will certainly not help sell your home. Find a new place for the pet's items and keep garbage away from the food.

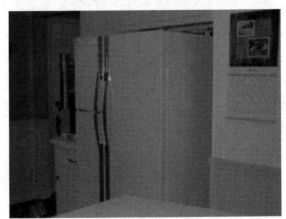

Refrigerator after uncluttering

After you get rid of the extra items, you still need to organize. One way to make things more organized is to buy small, inexpensive storage containers with pull-out drawers.

One of the best advantages of cleaning out your pantry is that some of the extra space can be used to store the toaster that is no longer on the counter.

Beneath the sink is critical, too. Make sure the area under the sink is as empty as possible, removing all extra cleaning supplies. You should scrub the area down as well, and determine whether there are any telltale signs of water leaks that may cause a home buyer to hesitate to buy your home.

Finally, take a look at refrigerator clutter – both inside and out. A refrigerator looks big when it has smaller quantities of food. Keep this in mind when shopping. It is worth your time to go to the grocery store more often and buy only half gallon milk containers than to take up space and make the refrigerator seem smaller.

The front of your refrigerator will also need to be uncluttered. You may enjoy your children's or grandchildren's artwork, family photos, and the daily to do list hanging in plain sight, but potential buyers will not. When they glance over the kitchen, their eyes will stop on the refrigerator and they will see clutter – clutter equals loss of equity. Keep that in mind.

PROFESSIONAL BONUS TIP:

I tell people that they need to look at the front of the refrigerator and take off everything – even their cute little magnets.

Now let's move on to furniture clutter. Most kitchens have little furniture except for a table and chairs, and perhaps some bar stools. Even with such sparse amounts of furniture, you still have ways of reducing the cluttered feeling.

One of the definitions of clutter is that there is too much in too little space. Although you may need a large table and several chairs for your family or you like having the space for when family comes by, large tables often make a kitchen or dining area feel much smaller.

> ## PROFESSIONAL BONUS TIP:
>
> Remove extra chairs from the tables. Unless you have a massive space, you will not need more than four chairs around a table. Also remove extra leaves from the table to make the room feel larger.

Look at your dining room. Apply the same tips to your dining room table as well as your kitchen table. Also look at the other pieces of furniture. It is also suggested that you clear out your china cabinet down to a few simple pieces.

> ## PROFESSIONAL BONUS TIP:
>
> If the dining room has an oversized china cabinet, consider removing it, or if has a top and bottom, remove the top to open up the space considerably.

Look at wall clutter: photos, lampshades, and kitchen knick knacks that detract from the spaciousness of your kitchen. It is far better to have one large picture than several smaller ones.

Waging War on Bathroom Bedlam

Next to the kitchen, bathrooms are often seen as the next most important rooms of the house.

Take a look at your bathroom. If you are like most people, you will find half-used shampoo bottles, a jumble of hair accessories, a curling iron, foam curlers, several cans of shaving cream, tub toys, lotions, medication, books and magazines, oils, candles, toilet paper. The amount of stuff we store in our bathrooms is far greater than the storage capacity for these small rooms, especially, if like many bathrooms, there are only a medicine cabinet and a small vanity.

> ## PROFESSIONAL BONUS TIP:
>
> Get rid of all medication bottles. If a buyer sees medication bottles, they will believe that someone sick lives there. They will determine that they do not want to buy a house with germs.

The problem with many bathrooms is that they are too small or they have not been updated since the house was built. Bathroom remodels statistically give you the highest return for your dollar, but not if you need to sell your house now. (To learn more about remodeling, see Chapter 2.)

Your best bet in a small bathroom is to create visual space by drawing the eye away from cramped areas. This often comes down to ridding the bathroom of inevitable clutter.

Once again, as with the kitchen, buyers are going to open the closets, drawers, and cupboards. They are looking for storage space and for evidence of leaks under the sink. As you know from uncluttering your kitchen, the best

way to get rid of cupboard clutter is to box it up and haul it out.

Counters will be an issue as well – and often an even bigger issue than kitchen counters. Why? Because of the small area dedicated to counter space. The more the counters are filled up with "stuff," the smaller the counters will appear to the buyer. Crowded countertops will leave the impression that they will not have room for their own make-up, hair dryer, and shaving kit.

Linen closets are another source of clutter. Linen closets store linens as well as extra toilet paper, soap, and shampoo. Linen closets also store "excess."

You probably own several sets of sheets for each bed in your house. You more than likely also have good towels, raggedy towels, beach towels, and other assorted towels! What should you do? Remember the "more than half" rule and box up and store most of what you have inside!

Now that we have the counter and storage areas taken care of, let us take a quick look into the bathtub or shower. What do you see?

It is time to tidy up. First, look at the number of shampoos, conditioners, body washes, and soaps. Do all of them have to be there? The ones that are not in use need to be boxed up and moved out.

PROFESSIONAL BONUS TIP:

Put away all hygiene products and personal grooming products. When you have these visible, the buyer sees the area as your personal space. Remember, the goal is to let them visualize themselves living in the home, not you living in the home.

Do you have tub toys overflowing a basket or simply cluttering up the tub? Consider having your children take toyless baths while selling the house. If this simply cannot be done, then put the toys in a tote that can be easily moved before showing. You might also consider getting a shower caddy to get the bottles off the tub surface. Look for a caddy that does not invade the bathing space.

Visual clutter in a bathroom often comes down to color. Although I will not deal with wallpaper and flooring here (See Chapter 2), there are things you can do while in the uncluttering step of home staging.

Disorder in the Den and Living Room

After the potential buyers have assessed the kitchen and bathrooms, they are going to notice other details in the house. The general living space will be next on their list.

Can they fit in their existing furniture? Will the living areas be large enough to entertain? Will they be able to watch TV and still see out the sliding glass door? These are the kinds of questions that will run through their minds as they view these spaces.

Having disorderly living areas will give them the following answers:

Living room before

- No, my furniture will not fit. I would have to buy all new furniture. I cannot afford new furniture. This house is not right for me.
- No, I will not be able to entertain in this area. It is hardly large enough to hold my furniture, let alone any guests. This house is not right for me.
- No, I will not be able to put my entertainment center in this room without having to

Living room after uncluttering

This Could Be You: TAKE A LOOK!

Before (left)

After (above): Notice the angled chair and table, as well as vertical art that lifts the eye to the higher ceilings.

Before (left)

After (above): Once again, the furniture is angled and a small room feels larger.

put it up against the sliding glass door. I certainly would not want to do that. This house is not right for me.

To avoid these kinds of thought patterns, you will want your living spaces to feel open and clutter-free.

Many people have too much furniture in certain rooms — not too much for their own personal living needs — but too much to give the illusion of space that a home buyer would like to see. You will want to create seating areas that allow movement into and out of the room and that draw attention to large windows, a fireplace, or other amenities.

Bookcase before

Bookcase after

☝ PROFESSIONAL BONUS TIP:

Crowded rooms lack energy. Eliminate as much furniture as you can and keep simple pieces and a limited number of knickknacks. You are going to have to move them anyway, so you might as well start packing them up now. Remember, you are selling your space, not your things.

When there is too much to look at, the buyer's eyes wander aimlessly, more likely to focus on the crowded spaces than on the beautiful features. Remember, you are not selling your furniture or your home or your decorating style. You are selling them a home – their home – and to do so, you have to remove the excess.

Believe it or not, your room can also look too empty. If you have a large space with small-scale furniture, the room will look large and uninviting. It will appear as if no amount of furniture can fill it up. This is only made worse if all of the furniture is pressed up against the walls.

As with other rooms, you need to look for obvious clutter. Such clutter will appear on tabletops, bookcases, and the floor. You will also want to clear any clutter from built in cabinets.

You will also want to eliminate clutter on the walls. Wall clutter can consist of several small photos all bunched together on one wall or large prints on nearly every square inch. It is far better to have a few nice pieces of art in strategic places than having your walls covered.

PROFESSIONAL BONUS TIP:

If there is anything that is political or religious hanging on your walls, take it down. You do not want to have someone dislike your home for any reason. I equate this with talking to a stranger. You would not have a conversation with a stranger about politics or religion, so do not let your house have one either. You will need to tread carefully since even the American flag can produce unwanted feelings. You will also want to rid your walls of animal trophies, guns, and knives. Many people find these things offensive.

Now let us move to the floor, where clutter really thrives.

Have you ever walked into a house and noticed that there were throw rugs everywhere? They were in the entryway, in the hallways, in the living room, in front of the kitchen sink, in the bathroom in front of the toilet, in front of the sofa, in the middle of the living room. They were simply everywhere. This kind of hodge podge is clutter.

One large piece of art over the mantel draws the eye to the beautiful fireplace.

Buyers want to see your carpet or your hardwood floor or your linoleum. Most home stagers suggest removing all area rugs, unless you have a large area of hardwood where one rug is acceptable. Area rugs make spaces seem more crowded. Without them your floor plan opens up.

Take a look at your walls and windows. Long, dark curtains can make a room seem small and closed in. Tiny pictures in a large room can be overwhelmed and seem out of place. Large pictures on a small wall can draw too much attention. All of this leads to a feeling of clutter.

PROFESSIONAL BONUS TIP:

When you look at a room and you think it is perfect, take away one more thing.

Clutter in the Closets

It is easy to hide clutter behind closed closet doors, but here is what a cluttered closet looks like once the door is opened.

Closets are great for accumulating clutter, though you may not think of it as clutter. Perhaps the clutter is wrapping paper, Christmas items, an old sewing machine, keepsakes, photo albums, extra clothes, and shoes. None of these things are likely to be in the throw away pile, but they should not be in your closets if you want them to look uncluttered.

People will open your closets. What are they going to see? If you unclutter, they will see an organized space. If they are not clutter free, no one would believe that their things will fit in the closet since your things obviously do not.

Closet before uncluttering

Why does your closet end up a cluttered mess? It is simple: in everyday life, it is one of the last places anybody sees! Even you probably do not see the closet clutter often. Plus, we grow attached to our items, and instead of throwing away something we no longer need, we hold on to it and store it just in case we may need it again, sometime in the distant future. After all, you never know, right?

When you do finally take a good hard look at your closets, the thought of getting them organized may be a little overwhelming.

As American wealth grows, so does our desire to consume, collect, and sometimes even horde. An entire industry has blossomed to help people sort through their closets, desks, garages, and offices. Today there are approximately 4,000 members of the National Association of Professional

Organizers, some of whom get paid several hundred dollars an hour to help clients sift through and organize their treasures!

Instead of paying someone thousands of dollars to get your closets organized, follow a few simple tips to do it yourself.

Begin by taking everything out of the closet. Do not worry about sorting the items into categories just yet. After the closet is emptied, clean it. Vacuum the carpet or clean the floors as needed. Scrub the walls down. Do not forget to wipe down the shelves.

Now it is time to look at the clothes. Here are three main questions to ask:

1. Does it fit?
2. Does it look good on my body shape?
3. Have I worn it in the past year?

If you answered no to any of the three questions, it is time to give the clothing item away to charity. Do this for all your clothes. This includes underwear, socks, nylons, belts, scarves, and pajamas. Be bold and only keep items that look great on you and that you can wear comfortably.

Now colorize. This makes your closet look appealing. Put the whites together; creams together, tans, pinks, reds, blues, and so on. Go from light to dark with the blouses, pants, skirts, and dresses.

The truth is men and women wear 20 percent of their clothes 80 percent of the time, and the average American male has 14 pairs of shoes; the average female 21. Ask yourself, how many different pairs have I worn in the last six months? You should have spring/summer clothes together and fall/winter clothes together. The off-season clothes should be put at the back of the closet and out of the way of the current season.

Now it is time to put the rest of your "stuff" back into your closet. As you go through your stuff, get serious and honest about each item. Ask yourself when you used it last. If it has been more than one year, toss it. If you only use this item once a year, try to store it in a more appropriate place. The main thing is to get rid of stuff.

When you run into something that has monetary value, consider whether it is worth your time to sell it. Online auctions and local antique shops are both great places to get rid of your clutter and make a little extra money along the way. When an item is not worth your time to sell, give it away or give it to a local charity.

If things still look a little cluttered, you need to purge more items.

Clutter Busters for the Bedroom

Bedrooms can be a dumping ground for all the things you do not know what to do with or where you dump stuff in a hurry for visitors. No one tends to see your bedroom except you or your partner, so you do not get the social pressure to tidy up as you do in the living room or kitchen.

However, when you are selling your home, bedroom clutter does matter! Start with first impressions. Stand a few feet away from the entrance to the bedroom. What do you see? Whatever you see is the first thing that a buyer

Bedroom in cluttered state   *Sewing table would be removed*

will see. Is it pretty? Is it bulky? Does it make the room feel small? Move anything from the doorway that is not inviting.

The most common bedroom clutter is furniture. Check your bedrooms to see if you have too many furnishings. Reduce furnishings to a bed, an end table or two, an armoire or dresser and a nice reading chair.

As I said earlier, my daughter's room is crammed full. You can see that there is an excess of furnishings as well as accessories. She loves her room, but buyers would not. Every inch of wall space is taken, and most of the floor space as well.

This room needs a big overhaul. Let's do a walk-through and see how the uncluttering process would work.

1. First, you would remove the sewing table. The table should go into storage and the sewing machine, if needed, can be placed on a closet shelf. All of the sewing odds and ends need to be boxed and stored.

2. For the dresser, get out a box and start packing. Messy dresser tops can make the room feel small. Get rid of photos, jewelry boxes, shells, and dolls. Find a piece or two that will draw the eye into the room.

 PROFESSIONAL BONUS TIP:

Reduce your contents and display simple items.

---

3. Posters on walls also need to go into storage. One large piece over the bed is enough.

4. Since the room has so much heavy furniture, I would put the bedside table in storage and put something small and light in its place – something with legs and no drawers. Removing the headboard would also get rid of the heavy look. I would also consider removing the bookshelf from the desk and storing it, along with its contents.

5. The shelf under the bookcase needs to have something of bulk that does not attract attention. A stack of three books or a larger accessory would work well.

Remove the top half of the desk, put knickknacks into storage, and put something on the shelf below.

6. The windows have no treatments. Although the window is large, there is nothing to draw the eye. A simple loop of material over the curtain rod can add color and depth, pulling the eye upward and onto the window. Be sure to open the blinds as well!

Remove the blinds and add a window treatment at the top of the window so that light may still come in.

7. Faded bedding draws unwanted attention to the bed, making it seem too large for the room. A cleaner, brighter quilt or comforter will allow the potential buyers' eyes to move across the bed without stopping.

Not all rooms need this much work, but understanding the uncluttering techniques will make any bedroom feel more spacious.

PROFESSIONAL BONUS TIP:

When staging a child's room, remove all posters and all but one stuffed animal. Stuffed animals can kill a sale because they are seen as clutter. If the buyer is not going to use that room as a child's bedroom, it is harder to imagine it as something else when it is filled with children's toys.

Spare Room Space

Most spare rooms are just that – spare. They are used for anything and often everything! It may be a guest bedroom and office. It may be a guest bedroom and storage room. It may be nothing more than a place to put things you have no other place for. More than likely, it is disorganized. And it will be a barrier to the sale of your home.

A spare room should be viewed as a bonus. It is a "plus" feature of your home, but only if buyers can view it as such. Clutter and disorganization will not help them see the room as it can be, but only as it is.

If you need this room as office space since you work from home, during the selling process you need to make it just that – an office! Get rid of the spare bed and the extra dressers full of last season's clothes. Get rid of the boxes of storage items in the closet. Keep the essentials of your office such as a desk, filing cabinet, bookshelf, and a nice chair in the corner with a small table and lamp.

The closet should be used for storing extra office equipment and supplies. Be sure that all supplies are neatly organized and on shelves – not on the floor. If you have always used the closet as a space to store extra clothes, put them into storage.

If the spare room is really a spare room plus a place to use your computer, you have two options. Either move the computer to a different location so that the room is truly a guest bedroom or get rid of the bedroom furniture and turn the room into a den with a computer. Turning the room into a "den" is often the easiest thing to do. Store the bedroom furniture and use some of the furniture you have taken out of the living room to create a cozy atmosphere.

When using this area as a den, you may want to consider using the closet as the computer desk area. Using file cabinets at each end of the closet with a sheet of plywood on top can make an inexpensive desk, or you can opt for a real desk. Do not forget the value of installing shelves above the desk for storage.

Front Entry Confusion

Although the kitchen is the first thing that buyers say they look at, the truth is that they SEE the front entry long before they get to the kitchen. You will want this area of your home to create a positive first impression. What they see in the front entry will give them a feel for what they will see in the rest of the house. A tidy entryway is key to making your home feel warm and welcoming.

If they see (and smell!) a stack of shoes, an umbrella stand overflowing with multi-colored umbrellas, and a faded wreath on the wall, they certainly will be uninterested from that point. If the entryway impression is so poor that the experience taints the rest of the home, the buyer will find nothing right.

What is crucial is that everything that requires a place has one, and items that do not belong are not just sitting there. Make sure there is room for free and easy entry to your home, and some mobility around the front door, whether it is open or shut.

After you have the entryway clutter under control, consider hanging a piece of art that tells the buyer something about what they will see in the rest of the home. It is important to make your décor as consistent as possible from room to room. If your entryway leads into the living room, the two decorating schemes need to flow together. Otherwise, you create a visual distraction.

Storage Area or Catchall?

One of the things a buyer considers when looking at a home is the storage it offers. The problem is that as we live in a home, these areas seem to become collection bins. Basements, garages, attics, storage rooms, laundry rooms, and sheds accumulate not only clutter, but junk. These areas should be as empty as possible so that buyers can imagine what they would do with the space. Remove anything that is not essential.

PROFESSIONAL BONUS TIP:

Whenever possible I recommend leaving the garage free from storage. If people see that the seller does not have enough storage and has to use the garage, they will begin to wonder if the same thing will happen if they buy the house. People like to think that they might actually be able to use a garage!

Since you are getting ready to sell your house, it is well worth investing time to conquer garage clutter and keep your garage organized and user-friendly. For busy families, the garage often becomes home to everything no longer wanted or needed inside the house. But like multiplying rabbits, garage clutter can quickly evolve into a tangled mess, leaving little or no room for the garage's intended purpose: a safe place to park your car.

Are you aware that about 90 percent of garages have no room for a vehicle? This is true no matter how big or small the garage. I have seen one, two, three, even four-car garages so packed with stuff that a tank could not ram its way in. Expensive cars often sit in the weather instead of in the garage, or broken down cars sit in the garage collecting boxes and other clutter.

What is wrong with that, you ask? Can you imagine what a prospective home owner thinks about a garage stuffed to the gills? "Where will I park my car?"

Now before you get all upset about a garage only housing cars, it is true that it is appropriate to store some things, like garden tools, sports equipment, and the lawnmower in the garage. Garages also make good space for workbenches and tool chests, but the garage should not be used as a dumping ground for whatever will not fit in the house. Your garage is not the landfill.

Some stuff does belong in the garage, but it does not belong on the garage floor where it can get run over, tripped over, and dirty. To get stuff up off the garage floor, I recommend peg-board and hooks, available at your local hardware store, for storing a variety of items. Peg-board is your garage's best friend. It is cheap, easy to hang, keeps things accessible, and it gets stuff out of the way.

For storing seasonal items and mementos such as the Christmas ornaments, Halloween costumes, and family photos that must stay in the garage, I recommend sturdy plastic storage bins, available at any discount store. Better yet, take those items in storage bins to your storage unit. The less you have in the garage, the larger it will appear.

PROFESSIONAL BONUS TIP:

Do not store packed boxes in the garage. The garage needs to feel open and roomy.

Designate one entire day to attack the garage. By the time that day rolls around, you should already have purchased pegboard, hooks, racks, and plastic storage containers. You will also be equipped with a broom and plenty of trash bags. No running around that morning to buy those things. Today you will spend only in the garage.

We have all heard the riddle, "How do you eat an elephant?" with the answer being "One bite at a time." The same approach holds true for your garage. One of the cardinal rules for any organizing project you undertake is to break the project down into small, manageable pieces.

The first thing you will do is to take everything out of the garage. That is right. Everything. Every box, bike, tool, pile of junk, and grandma's Art Deco vanity you are going to refinish someday—it all goes into the driveway. Then you attack with the broom. Sweep out all the dust, leaves, cobwebs, and bugs.

When the garage is spotless, attach the peg- board to the walls and erect the workbench, if needed.

When that is done, it is time to go through all the stuff. Sort through each box, bag, and mound, and make three piles of stuff.

Pile one is stuff that is going to go away. Garbage, recycling, and things to be donated go in this pile. Broken items, scraps of wood, rusty tools, parts of appliances, electrical equipment that no longer works are all candidates for the recycle bin, trash bin, or Goodwill. Fix it, use it, or let it go. Emotionally speaking, this will be the hardest job of the day. Do not let sentimentality trip you up here.

Pile one also includes empty boxes. I see too much space eaten up by empty boxes. You do not need them. If you are keeping them for "someday," do not. Empty boxes are a dime a dozen. If you need some, all you have to do is drop by a liquor store, restaurant, or retail shop on shipment day, and they can fill your car with boxes. Break down your boxes and ship them off to be recycled.

Pile two consists of those things that only get used once or twice a year. Holiday ornaments, Halloween costumes, and family photos should be packed in plastic containers.

Pile three includes thing that get used often   gardening tools, bike pump, soccer ball, and bicycles.

Reality Check

✓ Imagine an $800,000 home with a huge double entry. You walk into a spacious foyer and look to the right expecting to see a big, beautiful living room and you see......car parts. Car parts! The owner worked on cars as a hobby and kept his old, greasy car parts in the living room. And they had been showing their house this way!! What they did is what so many people do. He liked his car parts there and figured that people could come in and say, "Of course. This is the living room." The owners believed strongly that buyers would be able to understand that this room filled with car parts was, indeed, a living room. The truth is, that in the end, the potential buyers can only remember the car parts. They were adamant that they were not going to come down on the price. They took some big suggestions and got rid of the car parts and the paint and wallpaper and got their price after just two months.

How are you storing your items? Be sure that all storage items are in the proper storage areas.

When the piles are made and the fate of all your garage clutter decided, start putting stuff back into the garage. Pile three goes on the peg-board or on a designated shelf or rack, pile two goes to your storage unit, and pile one goes away.

The last task of the day is to park your car in the garage. Your garage will look much bigger to a potential buyer, create a positive feeling about how the house has been maintained, and allow you quick and easy access to stored items.

Now take a quick look at your attic and other storage areas. Much of the same advice about garages applies here as well. Take everything out of the attic (or other storage area) and make the three piles. Let go of those old love letters, broken chairs, 10 year old tax records, old baby clothes, rugs, useless tools, old towels and sheets, extra blankets, and anything else you no longer need. If you have not used it for the past two years, chances are you do not need it, and perhaps someone else could make use of it.

Be sure to box up items that you will not need during the sale of your home and ship them off to your storage unit. Just as uncluttering made your garage appear larger, so will it make your attic, storage rooms, laundry rooms, and sheds appear larger.

Make sure these areas are well organized and give prospective buyers the impression that there is room for all their belongings. Do not let a perceived lack of storage space become an objection.

CASE STUDY

Staging itself is based on the need of the home. Every home has the ability to be staged. It might just be a consultation where a home enhancer goes through and shares thoughts, or a home enhancer may be more like a project manager and be involved in redoing a kitchen, picking out colors, or landscaping. If the home is higher priced, there may be more things you need to do to make it look like a model home, but all homes can benefit from staging.

Some stagers who have never seen your home can see it through a potential buyer's eyes. They can see the things that need to be changed. They know what else is on the market. They know what they can do to help the home owner based on the market.

Many home owners find the process of staging a bit difficult because I am walking into their biggest investment as well as their personal space. I have to share with them right up front that what I am doing is not personal. I help them  realize that once they put their home on the market, it has to appeal to the most people. I need to help them get their mind out of the home.

As a stager, you really have to get the view of the home owner. The best way to help them through this process is to ask if there is anything they would feel uncomfortable changing. I let them know that it is not easy and I thank them for letting me come into their home. Once they see that I am there to help them sell their home, they grasp the idea and are able to make the changes that are needed to achieve this goal.

Sometimes renovations are needed, especially if they want a certain price for the home. Certain renovations almost always get your money back. For instance, a renovated kitchen will add enough to the asking price to pay for the renovation. The same goes for bathrooms. However, it really does depend upon how much you put into it. For instance, if you are in an area that granite counter tops will put you well above the rest of the comparable homes in the area, you may not be able to recoup your costs. This is where it is really necessary to consult with your realtor to determine what renovations will recoup and which ones will not.

I believe in having a home inspection done and fixing those items that you know will be inspected. If you are going to do them, you may as well do them now. Have them done and fixed appropriately so that they will know what has been taken care of. This has the added benefit of making the house looked well cared for, and well cared for homes sell faster.

If you are trying to sell an empty home, you certainly do not want to leave it empty as you put it on the market. I think that staging the main living spaces such as the living room, den, dining room, and master bedroom is essential. The whole house does not need to be furnished as long as these areas look inviting. You do not even need a full set of furniture in these rooms. You can have something like a bistro table and two chairs in the kitchen or a bed and side table in the bedroom. However, if you have not painted the walls and put in new carpet, staging will not be of much help. A vacant home will show the carpet and the paint even with a bit of furniture!

There. You have now uncluttered your home. Your shelves are clean, your drawers are organized, and the bookcases and tabletops have just the right amount of knickknacks. Keep clutter to a minimum to truly showcase the spaces you have.

So, what is next?

Depersonalizing!

General Uncluttering TIPS

87. Look around your house. Begin a list of the items that you no longer use, are disorganized, make things too crowded, or are unfinished. This is where you will start when uncluttering.

88. One of the best ways that I have found is using the clutter criteria listed at the beginning of this chapter. If it has not been used, is disorganized, makes things too crowded, or is unfinished, it needs to go. Sometimes, of course, this cannot happen. A disorganized bookshelf may not be able to be moved, but you can organize it

and use the criteria to determine if everything on the shelf needs to stay.

89. Even if you only work 1 to 2 hours a day, complete whatever process you have begun. If you have started on the kitchen counters, finish that before ending. Do not forget to do something with what you have moved. (See Tip 4)

90. Find out what organizations in your area pick up items. Such organizations often include Goodwill, The Salvation Army, veteran's associations, and other local organizations. Another good way to get rid of items you no longer need is to use The Freecycle Network, a non-profit organization with more than eight million members around the world, with links to active groups in all 50 states. Here, you can list items you no longer need and then choose someone from a list of takers to have them. The best part is the person wanting the items comes to your home on your timetable to get them. You can find a freecycle group in your area by going to www.freecycle.org.

91. Rent a storage unit or borrow a friend's garage for a few weeks or months and fill it with boxes of collectibles as well as sports equipment, holiday decorations, seasonal clothing, and extra furniture.

Kitchen Uncluttering TIPS

92. Get everything off the counters. Everything. Remove all appliances from the countertops. Even the toaster. Doing so will make you kitchen look larger and more spacious. It will also keep the buyer's eye from stopping on a particular item rather than getting a full view of the room. Put the toaster in a cabinet and take it out when you use it. Find a place where you can store everything in cabinets and drawers.

93. After removing everything from your counters, you may find that you do not have enough room in your cabinets to put everything.

Clean them out. If you have dishes, pots, and pans that rarely get used, then put them in a box to go to a storage unit.

94. Get rid of the junk in your junk drawer. If you feel you may need some of that "junk" then get a small box that you can tote right out of the kitchen before prospective buyers come for a visit.

95. If you have a large amount of foodstuffs crammed into the shelves or pantry, begin using them. Let what you have on the shelves determine your menus and use up as much as you can. Or box some of those canned goods up. Canned goods will last in storage and you can use them once you get to your new home.

96. Your pantry can become a catchall. When uncluttering your pantry, remove anything that is not kitchen related.

97. Keep all wastebaskets out of sight. A good place to keep a wastebasket is under the sink. Even if you typically use a large wastebasket in the kitchen, change to a smaller one for the selling process. This will make your home seem cleaner and fresher and will be one less item in the kitchen.

98. Rather than store items in mismatched plastic containers, get a set of matched containers to place items like sugar, flour, rice, etc.

99. Storing a few big items in place of lots of little items will make the pantry feel less cluttered and far more spacious.

100. Other ways to create space in your refrigerator are to use plastic storage bins to

keep meats and cheeses out of view as well as neatly organized, buy smaller containers of condiments, use spacers in your door to leave room between groups of bottles, and buy smaller quantities of foods such as eggs, vegetables, fruits.

101. Clear refrigerator fronts of messages, pictures, etc.

102. Any important, needed information that you typically post on the front of your refrigerator can be stored on the side in a neat manner.

103. Remove the center leaf from the table to make it much smaller.

104. Try repositioning the table, perhaps at an angle, to open up more space. Areas with smaller spaces may need to have the table pushed up against a wall to provide a feeling of more floor space and flow to the area.

105. If you have an average sized space, remove all but four chairs from the table. If you have a smaller space, remove all but two chairs.

106. Barstools are nice, but can cause flow problems and make the room seem small. If you have barstools with backs, considering removing them and replacing with inexpensive wooden ones that will slide up under the counter. Keep the number of stools down to create a feeling of openness.

Bathroom Uncluttering TIPS

107. Tackle one area at a time, starting with the area under the sink or the medicine cabinet   major bathroom-clutter hot spots. Remove everything and sort into groups of similar items: shampoo with shampoo, cosmetics with cosmetics and so on.

108. Pack up ½ to 2/3 of what you have in your cupboards and put it into storage. Realistically speaking, how many towels do you need in a week? That is all you need to store in the bathroom.

109. Use bins to store personal care items. Instead of having a drawer full of make-up, you can have a nice storage bin with the make-up, thus leaving the drawer spacious feeling.

110. To prevent counter clutter, keep your most needed and used items, such as make-up, brushes, etc in one container that can easily be put in a drawer or shelf before showing your home.

111. If you need more space in the bathroom, you might want to consider adding a small corner shelf to hold fresh towels or even pretty storage containers of lesser-used items.

112. If your bathroom has a linen closet, be sure that all towels and sheets are neatly folded. It would be a nice touch to have the colors coordinated. If you have an odd assortment, consider buying a storage bin to "hide" them from prying eyes while making your linen closet look neat and tidy.

113. Store bottom and top sheet, with spare pillowcases into one pillowcase to lay flat.

114. Other clutter collectors include the top of the commode, tubs, and shower stalls. Keep only the most needed items in the bathtub.

115. If you already have a caddy, then be sure that it is sparkling clean. If it does not clean up, investing in another caddy will help make your tub look clean and fresh.

116. Coordinate towels to one or two colors only.

117. Small areas, such as bathrooms, need small pictures on the wall. Large pictures overwhelm the room and make it feel even smaller than it is.

Living Room, Family Room, and Den Uncluttering TIPS

118. Remove any unhealthy plants to create a good first impression.

119. As a rule most home owners need to remove about 1/3 of their furniture and accessories before showing their home.

120. You may want to tour some builders' models to see how they place the furniture. Observe how they place furniture in the models so you get some ideas on what to remove and what to leave in your house. If you do not have time to physically tour model houses, you can save time by accessing photo sharing social media web sites like Pinterest.com and subscribe to Really Simple Syndication (RSS feeds) from home owners and builders who share their staging photos online. Many photos on Pinterest include before and after pictures so you can see the difference that proper home staging makes.

121. Be sure that your furniture is not blocking any walkways or entrances, or overshadowing the nice features of your living room like built-in bookcases or a fireplace.

122. Try many different arrangements of furniture in groupings to see what works best for your living spaces.

123. For large rooms that appear too empty, try adding a tall, bulky piece of furniture. There is no need to spend a lot of money. Try looking at thrift stores or garage sales.

124. Remove any large or bright artwork from over the fireplace. Doing so takes the attention off the artwork and onto the fireplace.

125. Be sure that the pictures or other wall decorations are not too small for the area or too high. Most home decorators suggest a height of 66 inches from the floor to the center of the picture.

126. Remove any excess accessories. You may enjoy having a mantel full of photos and candles, but one or two items will add to the feeling of spaciousness and give the buyer a chance to visualize their own items there.

127. Unclutter your shelves. Clutter on the shelves gives the buyer the feeling that you do not have enough storage space. Once again, remember the ½ to 2/3 rule.

128. Remove all paperback books from your bookshelves and pull all the books flush with the edge of the shelf.

129. Throw rugs over carpet make buyers wonder what you are trying to hide. Could it be that the carpet is old or frayed? Never leave the buyer wondering.

130. A few bold accessories will help focus the buyer's eyes into the right places in your living room or other living spaces. Lots of accessories will make the same space feel cramped.

Closet Uncluttering TIPS

131. It is an easier task if you have a friend or family member join you to take a long, honest look at your wardrobe.

132. Do not use the "free" wire hangers. Instead, get some nice plastic tubular hangers that are all the same color. You would be

surprised how that makes a huge difference in a first impression of your closet.

133. Consider storing clothes from a different season in your storage building. If it is summer time, there is no need to have winter clothes and coats taking up space.

134. A hanging shoe-storage rack is perfect for organizing your shoes, and it will keep them off the floor as well.

135. Do you have anything that is torn, that you have not thrown away in the hopes that you will stitch it up? If this is the case, then sit down immediately, stitch it up and wear it the same or next day. If you cannot see yourself doing this, throw it away.

136. Do without excess items for a couple of months by putting them in a box. These items can make your closets look "crammed full."

137. Remove 2/3 of hanging clothes (there is that rule again.) and keep floors clear.

Bedroom Uncluttering TIPS

138. Look behind the piece of furniture that you see from the doorway. If you have stored flat items behind it, remove them. If you have a tangle of cords, detangle them and hide them from view.

139. Remove excess accessories. Box these up and put them in storage.

140. Remove headboards and mirrors attached to dressers to give the room a more spacious feeling.

141. Remove extra blankets at the end of the bed or in the closet. These can go into storage, or at least put in under-bed storage containers.

Office Uncluttering TIPS

142. Be sure to keep your desk neat and papers organized. If you are not good at keeping your papers organized, then have a tray or folder handy for showings. You can put all papers into the tray and store the tray away in a desk drawer or in the filing cabinet.

143. Another alternative is a less expensive mobile computer cart that could be rolled out of the room (or into the closet) when guests arrive. You might also want to replace your laptop or desk computer entirely with a mobile smart phone or an iPad.

Front Entrance Uncluttering TIPS

144. Be particularly careful not to hang or pile things behind the front door. Having to fight your way in the front door will definitely lead to negative first impressions.

145. To find the ideal place on the wall, walk through your front door and notice where your eye lands first.

Garage and Other Storage Area Uncluttering TIPS

146. Things that are used often should be hung from pegboard —tools, gardening accessories, electrical cords, skates, bicycle helmets, ski poles, flashlights, just to name a few items.

147. For skis, snowboards and bikes, purchase special hangers or racks, which will keep those things stored safely.

148. Consider removing items such as skis, sleds, bikes, yard equipment, etc. to the storage unit as well.

149. Label all storage containers in detail so you will not always need to open them.

150. Haul the "trash it" pile to the dump, recycling center, and/ or donation station that day—do not put it off. If you do not have the proper vehicle for hauling, make arrangements beforehand to borrow one or have a local hauler come to take it away to its destination.

151. Use walls to create more storage space without using up precious square footage.

152. Painting the walls of a garage or storage area will make the area feel fresh and spacious.

153. Be sure to check your automatic garage door safety reverse mechanism. It should stop and reverse even if it hits a roll of paper towels. If it does not, it needs to be adjusted.

Chapter 5

Take the Home Out of the House

Defining Depersonalization

A buyer makes the decision to buy your home in the first few seconds after crossing the threshold. The view as you enter a home is the most important one. Staging, theoretically erases the home owners' personal fingerprint from the home, making it a bit more generic. This enables the buyer to envision themselves living in that home, as soon as they enter it.

When "depersonalizing," the key word is anonymous. The house must look like it could be anyone's home. When a potential buyer is previewing your home, your real estate agent is selling the idea that this can be their home. Too many personal items of the seller lying around and it may hurt these chances.

The way you live in a home and the way you sell a home are two very, different things. You are selling a house that will become someone's home. You are not selling your home to someone. It is a subtle difference but one that needs to be understood. You want your house to evoke feelings of home to the buyer – their home, not yours.

The typical buyer will have trouble picturing themselves living in your house. It is hard to imagine living anywhere that someone else currently lives. If you keep your precious items out, the potential buyer may like them and even oooh and ahhh over them, but they will not buy the house. Why? Because it will not feel like their home. They will not be able to get past your personal style.

When it comes to selling your home, there is one main thing you need to take out – you. Not you physically, but the things that make the house YOUR home. Although the buyer probably will not notice that the home has been depersonalized, they will notice if it has not been.

By creating a depersonalized, open, and inviting space, you allow the buyers to focus on the unique features of your home. You also allow them to mentally move in without being distracted by your personality.

Reality Check

There it was. A large home on a golf course. It was on the market for $928,000. As you entered the home, you found yourself in a large open foyer with the stairs leading up to a large loft area. Right on the banister hung a huge mirror with a silhouette of a woman and the words "Sexy Mama." Stunned. That was the only words buyers could use to describe their feelings upon seeing it! There was no way to get it down without a lot of hard work because of the height and the way it had been mounted. The solution? Hanging a piece of artwork over it so that it was no longer visible!

Do you have any questionable art on display? Even things like military awards and religious books can offend some people.

Keeping the Personality: A Classic Example

Here is what Gail Greer had to say about a friend who was selling her home and failed to depersonalize:

> A friend of mine who lives in another state put her house on the market. Initially she had several showings. However, she learned the hard way that since she was SO creative and had SO much beautiful furniture and her own designed décor (which was gorgeous), the potential buyers were more attracted to *her things* than the house. It is a large home and the buyers got the "emotional"

message (acknowledged or not) that they did not have enough furniture and decor to fill the house.

They kept asking her questions about how she made some of her decor. The sale of the home became secondary to her amazing talents. No offers were received. My friend learned a valuable lesson.

Her house was seen as a show place instead of a home where they could imagine their furnishings.

Her home has been on and off the market for almost a year now. She is discouraged and has removed much of the furniture and accessories. Her home still has a homey appearance, but potential buyers can now imagine visualizing their things in that home.

She recently said to me, "I just wish I had known sooner. I would have done all this before and not put the house on the market until it was really ready like it is now. What a difference! It is a GREAT home!"

This Could Be You:
A Real Estate Agent Success Story

I had clients whose entire home was decorated in Americana. They were proud of their home, but it was overly done. They had colonial trim and hardwood floors. Everything had the dark wood and there were hundreds of knick-knacks, even lining up the staircase. They were on their second

real estate agent and could not understand why the house was not selling. They were also in trouble because they had already purchased a new home and could not make the house payments on both homes. They were nearing foreclosure.

The wife had a lot of difficulty making any changes, but her husband was a bit more receptive. However, as she saw what I could do in a room, she warmed up to the idea, especially since I did not force anything on her. I agreed to leave their master bedroom the way it was and she agreed to allow me to stage the downstairs and the stairway. Staging made a huge difference.

We took new photos of the home and they had offers within three weeks! They got their asking price and were able to stop the foreclosure on their new home.

CASE STUDY

Every home can use staging to its advantage. What home cannot use a little sprucing up? What home owner would not do a little something to dress up their home to make the sale? I can stage a 2000 sq. ft., three-bedroom, two-bath home for $300 to $500. Why would you not spend that money to sell your home for thousands more?

Staging is all about depersonalizing and broadening the appeal to a larger target. For me, the key word here is to depersonalize. You have to get the home owner to realize that this is not a home but a house. It is a property to be sold. You have to get them to cut the umbilical cord. To do this, you have to put away all the family photos. You do not want the buyer to come in and see who is living there. You want them to see themselves living in the house.

Packing away these photos ruffles the most sellers' feathers. People love their homes, as they should! But when it goes on the market, it is show time. You need to let someone else mentally move into the house. When you can take the owner out of the home, you can then focus the buyer's attention on the features of the home. You want them to see the fireplace or the French doors. You want them to notice all the features the home has to offer.

I definitely recommend a lot of updating, especially for certain homes. A real estate agent will know the market better than anyone. They know whether a kitchen needs to have some work!

For instance, I know of an older home that was listed for $334,000. It was on a golf course and had a tennis court, but brand new homes with granite counter tops and Berber carpets were selling for the same price. This home sat for 90 days with no contract. Then they brought me in. I had them put in granite tops, update the paint, and update the carpet to compete in that market. The owner spent $8,000 for the work and upped the asking price to $358,000. They definitely will get their money's worth. These updates took the home up a notch and helped it compete with the newer homes!

To me, all of my staging efforts have been success stories. What family wants to put their life on hold? If I can help them sell their home quickly and for more money, whether they have an $84,000 home or a $499,000 home, it is a success!

If I had to name one thing to do to a home, it would be fresh paint. You get the most bang for your buck with a bucket of paint.

The next thing I would suggest is to pressure wash the front of your house. This is where the buyer stands the longest. They are formulating an opinion! Also, be sure to change out that rusty porch light fixture or the dull and dirty doorknob.

I try to create rooms that a buyer can see themselves in. For example, I have a small two-bedroom, one bath home with 1500 square feet for sale. I will stage the master bedroom and stage the second room as an office and a guest room. I am doing the thinking for the buyer. I am showing them how much home their money is going to buy them. The key to staging a smaller home is to create dual spaces out of a smaller space.

When you have a home with more bedrooms, you have the luxury of using one or more of those bedrooms for a specialty room, such as a toy room, a separate den, or a study. I just do the thinking for the buyer. They want to get into a house. They do not like the home-buying process. They are going to make the offer when they can see themselves in the house.

Staging an empty home is different from staging an occupied home. My way of handling this is to address certain rooms. I stage the kitchen and the bath, and then any features like a beautiful fireplace mantel.

I want a buyer to go "AHHHH" and if I do not hear that, then I did not do my job right. If you can get that, it is an emotional attachment. If you can get that emotional attachment as they walk through the door, you have a better chance at a sale.

Erasing Your Imprint

Here are several things to do to de-personalize your home. Remove:

- Family portraits
- Drawings by the children
- Trophies
- Awards
- Vacation souvenirs
- Family treasures
- Personal quilts or wall murals

Pack them away.

By removing these personal things from the house or from view, you are really giving the buyer "permission" to move their things into, and to "buy," the house mentally. Until they can do that, they will never make an offer.

This Could Be You: A Real Estate Agent Success Story

There was one house in which the kitchen was a problem. The home owner had been trying to infuse color into the kitchen, and she had her upper cabinets painted green and her lower cabinets painted an eggplant color. I made a change so that everything was white. The cabinets were white. The counters were white. The floor was white. Then I added black and white photos and red spots of color with accessories. The home owner, upon seeing the updates, replied, "This is what I have been trying to do in this kitchen for four years and you did it in a day with accessories!"

Another thing to consider removing is a theme. Is your house country? Or Colonial? Or French provincial? You may want to remove as many items as possible that reflect that theme. If a prospective buyer does not like "country," they may be turned off by your accessories and never really see the house and all its features.

Reality Check

There was a home that needed to be staged, but it was infested – not with fleas or rodents, but with a teenage son! He had taken over the entire house. One room stored his Sony Playstation and video games. Another room housed his musical instruments and stereo equipment. His shoes were all lined up in the front hall. The garage was filled with sports equipment. The house screamed "teenager." The challenge here was to get the rooms functioning as they did before the teenage takeover. Although he was not happy with the new living arrangements, the house sold quickly!

Have you let something take over your house? It could be a child, a pet, or even a hobby. Be sure to depersonalize your spaces so that others can move in.

Sterile Does Not Sell

No one wants to visit a home that feels sterile. A sterile home is cold and uninviting. When you are told to depersonalize, this does not mean that you create a cold environment. Can you still have color? Yes you can. Can you still have artwork? Yes you can. And you may even be able to keep a piece or two of a collection or even grandma's quilt – but it is all in the placement.

The whole reason you depersonalize the space is so that others can see themselves in the home. They will not do that with your photos all over the place and they will not do it in a cold and sterile environment. It is important to find a happy medium. That is why you need to place furniture and accent pieces strategically.

Reality Check

 To one stagers dismay, the clients had taken the idea of "uncluttering and depersonalize" just a bit too far. They had removed everything except the furniture. There were no knick knacks, no photos and nothing on the walls!! Prior to the 'cleansing' there had been more than enough art. The house looked empty! Keep in mind that uncluttering does not mean emptying your house of everything you own! You want your home to have a warm feeling and a bit of pizzazz. That cannot happen if there is nothing in the house! This is exactly why vacant homes needs to be staged.

Have you taken away so much that your home no longer has any sparkle? Although YOUR personality needs to be removed, the personality of the house still needs to come through.

You do not want a hodge podge of chairs in the living room. You do not want a bookcase full of souvenirs from your latest beach trip, including those shells that still have a bit of sand, not to mention the smell! But you do not want the living room to be so barren that it echoes, or the shelves to be so empty that they go unnoticed.

PROFESSIONAL BONUS TIP:

If a home does not show well in photos and virtual tours, buyers will eliminate it from their list. That is one reason why it is important to stage each room correctly using proper staging and decorating principles.

After you have uncluttered and depersonalized, you need to decorate!

Depersonalizing TIPS

154. Recent data shows that homes sell twice as fast when the seller's personal items have been removed.

155. Pretend that you have a delete button at your side. Go through each room and delete your personal items from each space.

156. Pack up those collections, no matter how much you love them. You do not want potential buyers studying your vintage collection of salt-and-pepper shakers rather than your house.

157. There should also be no pajamas on the back of the bathroom or bedroom doors or personal toiletries out in plain view.

158. Get rid of shavers, shampoo bottles, and clutter on the counter. Yes this is inconvenient but remember the goal of this is to get your home sold fast, so put up with short-term pain for the long-term gain.

159. Limit artwork that is personal or potentially offensive to more conservative buyers.

160. Use solid fabrics and neutral surfaces (walls, floors, and ceilings) to attract the widest range of potential buyers.

161. Neutral does not have to mean white. A neutral color can be golden, wheat, khaki, sage, or any other number of colors often named for nature. My favorite is river moss!

162. Limit bold colors and patterns to items that are not permanent. It is much better to have a bright purple pillow than a bright purple wall.

163. Check to see if your personal decorating style is appealing to both men and women. Floral patterns, pastel colors, and cute knickknacks may turn a man off, just as dark paneling, hunting gear, and sports may turn a woman off. Your personal tastes must be set aside and a gender neutral space needs to emerge.

164. Depersonalize does not mean sterile. Sterile homes and personalized homes have the same problem – they do not sell well!

165. When depersonalizing any space, do it in small steps. Take away a few items and then step back and take a look. If you take too much away, you will end up with a lifeless room.

Sample Staging...

Chapter 6

Putting It All
Back Together

One of the biggest staging dilemmas for do it yourselfers is how to arrange the furniture and accessories once you have removed them to do the cleaning, uncluttering and depersonalizing. You probably left your furniture in the room, but have taken out most of the other accessories and removed the wall hangings when you painted.

So, there you stand in your clean and fresh room – wondering what to do next! The first thing you need to do is understand the market.

Knowing Your Market

What is selling in your area? Who is buying? The answers to these questions will help you develop a room-by-room plan for designing your different rooms. I am sure you are wondering how this knowledge helps, so let me give you an example.

Let's imagine that you are in a neighborhood where the houses on the market all have three bedrooms and two baths. Your house has five bedrooms and three baths. Having one extra bedroom and bath is going to be a great selling point for your area. But five bedrooms is just overkill.

PROFESSIONAL BONUS TIP:

You need to know your market. For instance, in most areas a seven-bedroom home will not sell. However, if you market it as a four-bedroom home with an office, an exercise room, and a den, you will have far more success. Stage these rooms accordingly.

In a case like this, you will want to determine how to stage the fifth bedroom. Once again, look at the market. Who is buying? Is it the young married but single crowd? The married with small children crowd? The family of older children and teens crowd? The empty nester crowd? Each of these different "crowds" will want something different from that extra room.

This Could Be You:
A Real Estate Agent Success Story

I recently sold a house where the couple had never purchased a dining room table and used the area for their stationary bike. I had them move the stationary bike to an unused basement bedroom and set up an "exercise room." They then rented a dining room table to show how the dining room would be used. The house sold almost immediately.

Of course, it is impossible to make the room suit everybody that enters into your home, but knowing the main target audience will help you stage it to their liking. For instance, those with teens may like to see a TV bonus room or a computer room. Those with small children may want to see an exercise room – getting out of the house to get to the gym is much more difficult when the children are younger.

The point here is to remember that not everyone wants five bedrooms. It is better to determine what your buyers are looking for and giving it to them.

PROFESSIONAL BONUS TIP:

People are repurposing space usage based on the new way we live. It is a more casual life style that requires more multi-purpose living space. Help the buyer see the space as multipurpose without leaving them wondering what can the space can do.

Another important point to remember is that people are not visual by nature. They need to see what the room is going to be. In most cases, they cannot look at an empty space and see a bedroom or an office. They just see an empty space. It is the goal of staging to help the buyer see the potential of the room.

PROFESSIONAL BONUS TIP:

You cannot have a pool table in your living room, or other item typically not found in a living room, because the living room needs to scream what it is. Buyers do not understand the way the floor plan is supposed to be; they only understand what they see when they walk in the door.

Learning From the Decorators

Once you know what you room you are creating, it is time to go to work. There are many general ideas that can help you when putting your items back into the room. The point here is to think outside the box without creating clutter or getting too personal.

This Could Be You:
A Real Estate Agent Success Story

My best friend had a condo conversion that had been on the market for six months. It was vacant and I had not yet tried my hand in staging. She was my first test case and what a test it was! There were 4 other units for sale that were identical to hers and one was even priced $6,000 less. We staged the kitchen, the dining room,

Table

and the bathrooms. The first showing after staging was the new buyer for the home! The buyer looked at them all and said that he got a better feeling in the staged unit and could see himself living there – even spending an extra $6,000 to do so! And to make it even better, she was able to sell the dining room table we had constructed out of wine crates and corks!

The buyer called up a few weeks after the sale and wanted the table that had been in the dining room because it had the right feel to the room. That shows how deeply his emotions were attached to the staging!

One of the most important factors to consider when placing items into a room is the idea of transition. As your eye moves around the room, you do not want it jumping from place to place or piece to piece. The movement of the eye should flow – not bounce. To accomplish this, you want to avoid abrupt changes in height. As you will see later in this chapter, art is a great way to move the eye along the room.

PROFESSIONAL BONUS TIP:

Keep the five senses in mind when decorating.

You will also want to give each room a touch of the unexpected. This can be done with artwork placed in an unusual way, using a piece of furniture in a way that you normally would not use it, or adding a dash of color where the eye least expects to find it. Be creative. Use what you have on hand but think of unique ways to utilize the components of the room.

PROFESSIONAL BONUS TIP:

It is ok and even preferred to have one room a little bit out of the norm. This way, when the buyer leaves, they remember the house with the memorable room. They can say, "You remember, the house with the black and white backsplash in the kitchen." You do not necessarily want to do this to a major room, but do something a little bit off the wall for good recall. Keep in mind that you do not want that "off the wall" décor to be an obstacle to the sale!

The real key to a successful room is achieving a sense of balance and proportion with furniture and accessories. Follow the "like-with-like" rule of the thumb. Tall with tall, small with small, wide with wide, and narrow with narrow will guide you throughout the decorating process. Mimic the shape of each space you are decorating. For example, a sofa should be accessorized with horizontal art so you are complementing wide with wide.

PROFESSIONAL BONUS TIP:

To give interest to rooms, coffee tables, and mantels, be sure to vary heights. This means high and low, as well as in and out.

Do not forget to leave a place for the eye to rest. Do not be afraid to leave some spaces unadorned.

Also, pay attention to the shapes surrounding the areas where you are placing art and furniture. If you have a wall with multiple door openings, you would not want to place a tall narrow TV cabinet there. If you have a set of windows with multiple panes, do not hang a grouping of small pieces beside it.

PROFESSIONAL BONUS TIP:

When you stage properly, it gives people perspective on furniture size. It helps the buyer see what will really fit in the different rooms.

CASE STUDY

I am a firm believer in home staging. When you stage, you are staging the walls and floors of the home, whether that space be 400 square feet or 4000 square feet."

Of course, you will do different things with each home since each home is unique. Whether your home is modest or expensive, a good stager will deal with what you have. It is about positioning, furniture placement, colors, and placement of art. That is not to say that I do not occasionally bring in my own props – I do. It is usually bedding and linens. The props, however, are just props that help the buyer to see the features of the home. The idea is to show off the house in the best light possible. That is all that really matters.

As a stager, I consult with the home seller before actually staging. At this point I give them a list of things to do – a way of preparing for the staging process. In fact, I actually do a walk through of their property and have them make a list along the way. This way, there is no miscommunication about the needs. Nonetheless, sometimes they have difficulty, but not in the way you would expect. I have home sellers pack up too much stuff!!

If they pack up too much, then I do not have anything to work with. Many sellers take the idea of uncluttering and depersonalizing to such an extreme that I walk in to find an empty bookcase – totally empty! When this happens, I have to think outside the box. I have to "find" items to put back in the bookcase or back on the tabletop. Having less to work with is harder than having too much. It requires me to be far more creative! It is far easier for me to ask them to remove a few things while I am staging than to have to create something out of nothing.

The only other thing I would like to mention here is that sellers have to clean their home – from top to bottom. That means the carpets and the floors, the counters and cupboards, the bathroom and the kitchen, and all the nooks and crannies in the entire house. No amount of staging is going to hide a dirty home. And stagers do not clean houses; they just stage them. To have a really successful staging process, you need to start with a clean house.

In general, I do not require renovations because people do not get their money out of them. Of course, this depends upon the price of the home and what the neighborhood is like. If the home sits in a great neighborhood, but has a 1950s kitchen, something will have to be done. In most cases, though, something simple like updating counters or painting cabinet doors will make a huge difference without actually renovating the entire kitchen.

On the other hand, I do suggest repairs! If something is making your house look bad, then do something about it. Are your walls dirty? Then you will need to paint. Is the carpet beyond cleaning? Then you may need to add new carpet. Do you have linoleum pulling up in the kitchen? Fix it. Are there chipped tiles in the bathroom? Replace them. When it comes to repairs, I firmly believe that you should fix whatever is obvious. If you can see it, so can the home buyer.

Putting the Pieces Together

My favorite decorating tip is to look outside the box. You do not always need to use an item for its intended purpose. For example, do not just use a tablecloth for a table, make it a slip cover for your ottoman. It can save you lots of money and time when you purchase a tablecloth at a local chain verses buying yards of fabric and by purchasing the correct size it can become a no-sew project. Always keep your eyes open for new uses for everyday items.

PROFESSIONAL BONUS TIP:

Use an aquarium base and put glass top on it to use as a table under a window.

PROFESSIONAL BONUS TIP:

Do not feel bound by tradition. I have used a patio table in a kitchen with a sheet over it (to cover the legs) and put a pretty vase with fresh flowers in the center.

Look for other stable pieces of furniture to place in front of your sofa other than the standard coffee table. Try ottomans, a large chest, a chess set on a display, stacked futons.

This Could Be You:
A Real Estate Agent Success Story

The house I am doing right now is in a great neighborhood but has a funky space that is 6 x 17 feet. A previous owner enclosed the back porch. This room still had the original porch lights on the ceiling as well as a small white ceiling fan. It was also carpeted. When buyers came into the home, they would always remark that this was a weird room and that they had no idea what they would do with it. It was what they remembered about the house and that was not a good thing.

So I had my painter go in and take down the two lights and update the ceiling fan. Then I had him paint the ceiling a light blue. We pulled up the carpet and put down slate in a diagonal to make the room feel more spacious. Then I added a small bistro set and a small water feature. Now, instead of wondering what the seller had done to the porch, they could now see themselves sitting there with their coffee and watching the children play in the back yard. I could have put an easel in that room instead! What I did was help the buyer see the potential of the room. I did the thinking for them. All of these updates cost $160. The house, instead of sitting, sold quickly!

Put some pizzazz into your living room by arranging the furniture correctly. Here is one way to make that easier:

1. With a tape measure, find the dimensions of the room. Draw the outline to scale on graph paper. A typical scale is 1/4 inch equals 1 foot.
2. Mark anything that would affect your arrangement: outlets for electricity, telephone and cable; light switches; windows; doors that open into the room; space between windows; and sill height.

3. Make scale paper cutouts of your living room furniture and shift them on the room drawing as needed until a likely arrangement emerges.

4. Select a focal point for your room and subtly orient other furnishings and some lighting toward it. If there is a fireplace, it will nearly always be the focal point; other focal points might be bookcases or built-in shelving to house lovely collectibles, or a sofa with a striking painting on the wall above it.

5. Arrange the furniture in such a way that pieces viewed as a unit do not show dramatic variance in height and mass as the eye sweeps the room. When a high-backed chair is next to a low table, boost the visual height of the table by hanging a piece of art above it.

6. Set up cozy conversation areas. Examples would include two chairs separated by a low table, or two love seats facing each other. When creating conversation areas, keep furniture pieces close enough to each other so that people can talk easily.

PROFESSIONAL BONUS TIP:

Make simple little vignettes. Use a mirror that reflects out into the backyard with a couple of chairs and a chess set. The buyer will immediately say, "OH!"

This mirror reflects a beautiful table arrangement

This Could Be You: **TAKE A LOOK!**

Living room with no focal point

Living room with the fireplace as the focal point

7. Pull furniture away from the walls for more flexibility in creating conversation areas. For example, use a sofa to divide space in a room.

8. Position the sofa so it is at a non-perpendicular angle to any walls to create drama. Perhaps put an area rug and coffee table parallel to the sofa.

PROFESSIONAL BONUS TIP:

There are two times that you can angle furniture: In a square room and if a room already has an angle in it, like a corner fireplace or a bay window.

9. Allow a minimum of 18 inches (24 is better) for traffic lanes through the room. Lanes will probably meander if you have two or three conversation areas in the room.

10. Bring furniture into the room and away from the walls to avoid the doctor's waiting room look.

PROFESSIONAL BONUS TIP:

A properly staged home does not have all the furniture up against the wall. Try putting furniture in a V arrangement to get a bit of the decorator's touch

Here are a few other bonus tips concerning furniture placement that I received from the professionals.

1. If you do not have a bed, get an inflatable bed and put it on a platform. Be sure to get sheets and a comforter that make the room stand out.

2. In a bedroom, unless you have no other choice, you want to see the foot of the bed when you walk in. You do not want a bed

to cross the doorway because it blocks the flow and makes the room look smaller. It is better to see the foot so that you can see the pretty pillows.

3. If the master bedroom has a TV, it needs to be in an armoire, or otherwise camouflaged. We stage for women, and a TV is a romance killer in the bedroom.

4. Many people buy wicker furniture because it is light and inexpensive. The problem is that it looks cheap and should only be found in certain areas of your home. You can buy good looking furniture that is inexpensive. If you do use wicker, do not overdo it.

5. If you have a good view, do not block windows with furniture or heavy window treatments. If you look out over another building or wall, then use interesting window treatments that diffuse the view and then create a focal point on the other side of the room.

Reality Check

There was a nice home with a living room, family room, formal dining room, and much more. The dining room, however, was anything but a dining room! It had a tiny card table, children's toys, a television, and a recliner sofa. The chandelier hanging from the ceiling was entirely out of place. The room was quite cluttered and simply did not say "dining room" to potential buyers. The solution was to find a drop leaf table from another room, and create a simple dining room vignette. Now the chandelier was positioned over the table and it was obvious that the room was a dining room.

Do you have any rooms that are begging to be explained? Remember, the average buyer cannot imagine how the room should be used – so explain it to them with the right furnishings and accessories.

This Could Be You: **TAKE A LOOK!**

Living Room with poor furniture placement

Proper furniture placement

Hanging Around

> ### PROFESSIONAL BONUS TIP:
>
> If you do not have good artwork, take photographs of flowers and scenery and have it blown up and put in a frame. Old wallpaper samples can make great mats for framing. You can paint mats different colors or use a faux painting method to change their appearance.

The arrangement of pictures has as much impact as the pictures themselves, which means you must decide where to display the piece so that it receives the attention it deserves. You will quickly discover that there are seemingly endless ways to display pictures:

- Hang one large photo, or display several smaller ones in a group.
- Arrange a group up a stairway wall, or wrap it around an inside corner of the living room.
- Hang a photo off-center over a particularly long piece of furniture, such as a sofa, and balance it out with a planter or other decorative object at the other end.
- Hang small pictures in small areas, such as corners or hallways, and large pictures in wide-open space.

> ### PROFESSIONAL BONUS TIP:
>
> People tend to use little pieces of art on their walls. Instead, use large artwork – it makes the room look bigger. Not only that, but you do not have to worry as much about the arrangement.

The art you would like to show off most should be placed at the room's focal point--the place your eyes are drawn to when you enter. Think of every surface in the room as a personal art gallery and the walls as primary display space. How you live in the space determines the best placement.

Do you want to see the piece as you walk into the room? Or is it something you would like to view while sitting on the sofa?

PROFESSIONAL BONUS TIP:

Mirrors can be good and they can be bad. Properly placed mirrors can help people literally see themselves in the room. However, mirrors should rarely be put over the fireplace since these mirrors will often do not reflect any of the pretty features in the room. Look at what is reflected in the mirror more than where it is actually located in the room.

One of the frequently asked questions is how high should I hang the artwork? The answer depends on the artwork and the type of room. You have probably heard many people talk about "eye level" and, of course, that is different for everyone depending on how tall they are. So who has the correct eye level anyway? Good question. Before determining the eye level, however, it is important to consider the main function of a room.

If the room is primarily used by people who will be seated, it is a good idea to lower the pictures or art on the wall so that it is more comfortable for them to enjoy when seated. In most cases, if you center whatever you are hanging, whether it be a single image or a grouping, and place the center at approximately 54 inches above the floor you will achieve a pleasing look. However, if you are place the artwork over furniture of any kind, you want to place the base of the art or grouping approximately a hand span above the furniture.

> ## PROFESSIONAL BONUS TIP:
>
> For new homes, rather than add pictures to the walls and add nail holes, use easels to display the artwork.

Adding the Jewels To the Room

One of the biggest home decorating dilemmas is how to arrange your accessories, whether it be a bookcase, shelf, or tabletop. Following these rules will help you keep spaces from being cluttered while creating charming vignettes.

When arranging a space with accessories, keep in mind that the most important thing to avoid here is boredom. This has a lot less to do with the objects you choose than how you choose to display them. To keep an arrangement from putting you to sleep, keep a balance of similarity and contrast. The similar shapes, colors, and styles will give your buyer a feeling of harmony, while the contrasting accessories will add spice. You want a bit of both in your arrangement.

Next, you want to make sure that the items you are using are the right scale. I once had a beautiful lamp with a large and wide shade. I had it placed on the table beside my couch. A friend of mine once called it my white elephant. It did not fit the space. It was too large for the table, too large for the furniture next to the table, and it blocked the view of the artwork. Most people tend to use things that are too small for their surroundings however.

> ## PROFESSIONAL BONUS TIP:
>
> When you stage your home, all accessories should be at least basketball size or dinner plate size. Large items have a presence and little items feel like clutter. Do not use three knickknack items on the mantel, but one big one instead

Once you have chosen your objects for the space following the design principles above, it is time to layer and soften. Start with a larger, taller piece slightly off center. This will be the defining piece in your arrangement. Now work to the outer edges in layers. Add a taller background layer, a middle sized medium height layer, and your tiniest objects in the front. Keep the eye moving up and down as it purveys the arrangement from left to right for interest. Add some fabric or twisted ribbon to soften the edges of the shelf or table, to bring in color, and to highlight certain objects.

Above all, keep trying new combinations of items until you find an arrangement that works for you. And remember, if your arrangement still looks cluttered and lost, chances are you are trying to display too much.

> ## PROFESSIONAL BONUS TIP:
>
> Rule of three: In any room you should use three or five items in a grouping. Never use an even number.

Creating Colorful Combinations

One of the most common problems that can happen when staging is the single color theme, and a neutral one at that. One way to change this is to add some colorful accessories.

One of the easiest ways to create color is to add beautiful accent pillows to any room. Introducing a complementary accent color in a room can make a room "pop" and come alive. Accent pillows not only add color but texture and warmth as well. By adding throw pillows in a coordinating or contrast fabric to a couch chair, bench, or bed, you can transform your room and add instant warmth inexpensively!

> ## PROFESSIONAL BONUS TIP:
>
> A good accent color is red because it stays with you the longest. It is good to make an impact. Gray is the least favorite color – this is why unfinished block wall in a basement are so unappealing. Try to avoid this color at all costs.

Other ways to include color are by adding a throw, a rug, window treatments, a piece of framed art, or a tabletop accessory.

> ## PROFESSIONAL BONUS TIP:
>
> The more you can make children's rooms gender neutral, the better. For instance, make it less pink and purple for girls and less sporty for boys. In this way, the rooms will appeal to a wider audience. Buyers will be able to see the space as a guest bedroom or office or even for a different gender child.

General Designing TIPS

166 WHAT you have is not as important as HOW you arrange it.

167. Small changes can give your room a fresh, new look.

168. Redesign is like a jigsaw puzzle. You just have to know where the pieces fit.

169. Repurpose what you have. Take that antique dresser out of the spare room and put it in the dining room as a server!

170. Of all shapes, the triangle is the most pleasing to the human eye. It is a shape that will be repeated many times in your arranging process. Furniture, lighting, and accessories will all be improved with the benefit of triangular placement.

171. To make a room appear as large as possible: Stand in the doorway. If you can see through to the baseboard at the farthest point, you have the impression of length, and subsequently space.

172. Easy access to a room ensures that it will welcome people to come in!

173. Creating vignettes or groupings of decorative items versus spreading them around the space, makes rooms more interesting.

Furniture Placement Tips

174. You can have the most fabulous furniture in the world, but if it is not placed correctly, it will not feel fabulous.

175. An inverted "V" arrangement facing the focal point will give you a change of pace from the more standard arrangement configurations.

176. Compliment furniture and accessory lines with like shapes. For example, a rounded table with chairs that have rounded backs.

177. Look for ways to vary the heights of the furniture and the plants and the wall decor in a room to capture interest. Watch out for extreme height variations.

178. Use vertical space to help a room seem larger and more open. Position your furniture in interesting positions utilizing diagonal positioning when possible.

179. Avoid placing a chair by itself. Incorporate it into a grouping or use it with a side table.

180. If your sectional is making your conversation area seem too small, try pulling it apart and reconfiguring. Hide unfinished sides with end tables. Drape a throw over a single-armed section to disguise the imbalance.

181. Furniture that is small does not make a room looker larger—be sure that scale is appropriate.

182. Do not block entries or windows with furniture.

183. Do not line furniture up around the edge of a room.

184. Prevent indentations in your area rug when placing it over wall to wall carpet by placing four-inch floor tiles between the two rugs and under furniture legs.

Wall Art Placement TIPS

185. Watch out for hanging artwork all around a room, spreading it out to fill like soldiers standing at attention. It will be obvious that you are just trying to s-t-r-e-t-c-h what you have to fit. Better to leave some walls alone so the eye has a place to rest.

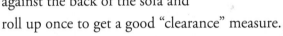

186. When hanging print art above a sofa, remember to leave arm space above the sofa back. A quick trick: lay your arm flat against the back of the sofa and roll up once to get a good "clearance" measure.

187. Oversized furniture calls for robust print art to strike a balance. For visual weight, consider a grouping of 2 or 3 prints that carry strong visual weight through color or a wider molding and mat combination.

188. When hanging art framed under glass, place a small piece of cork between the upper center of the frame and the wall to eliminate glare.

189. Treat the wall around a piece of furniture like matting on a picture. Let the wall frame your furniture or artwork. Do not fill the entire wall space – only fill 2/3.

190. Never hang anything over furniture where the width of the furniture is shorter than the width of what is on the wall. If you do it will feel top heavy. If you really need to hang something

wider over a piece of furniture, place something else next to the furniture so that what is below will visually support what is above it.

Color Decorating TIPS

191. Remember this easy trick the next time you are walking down the pillow aisle at your favorite home store: Pick up two pillows in a soft solid color, and then buy a third pillow with a bright pattern. This combo will keep your sofa neat and simple but with a twist -- like hanging a vivid painting on a beige wall.

192. Never underestimate the power of an area rug! It can add color, texture, and create a space within a space!

193. Greenery, live or artificial, will add life and warmth to any room. Consider displaying cascades of greenery from pots placed on decorative wall brackets or shelves.

Chapter 7

Take It Outside

Many people think of the interior when selling the home but neglect to unclutter, clean, and decorate the exterior. This is a big mistake since a home buyer's first impression is based on his or her view of the house from the real estate agent's car. This first impression is called curb appeal.

One way to see if your home has curb appeal is to walk across the street and have a good look at your house. This would be a good time to look at other nearby houses, too, to see how yours compares. After you have taken a good look, it will be time to go to work.

PROFESSIONAL BONUS TIP:

Many people drive by homes at night because they work during the day. Therefore, it is essential that you have nighttime curb appeal. If your home is dark, it is not appealing. Strive to make it the brightest house in the neighborhood. It will feel warm and appealing.

Curb Appeal Stops at the Front Door

When I had you stand across the street and evaluate your home, where did your eyes go? They should be drawn to the front door and entryway. If they are not, then you need to do something about it.

It may be as simple as cutting a few limbs so that the front door is visible. Remember, if the buyers cannot see your house, they will not buy it!

Other things that may keep the front door from being the focal point are peeling paint, crooked shutters, and general disrepair. Look critically at your house and see what catches your eye. Do you have a loose gutter or shutter that is hanging on to the house in a lopsided manner? This is the time to make a correction! Is the paint peeling or flaking on the house or is your vinyl siding dingy? These things will be noticed first and your front entryway will not create interest.

Once any repairs are made, there is one simpler thing to do to get your front entry way to show up first. You can paint the front door a bolder color than the rest of the house.

The front door should be especially sharp, since it is the entryway into the house. Polish the door fixture so it gleams. Make sure the lock works easily and the key fits properly. When a home buyer comes to visit your home, the agent uses the key from the lock box to unlock the door. If there is trouble working the lock while everyone else stands around twiddling their thumbs, a negative first impression hits prospective home buyers.

PROFESSIONAL BONUS TIP:

When a realtor comes up and jiggles the lock box, this is a signal that the buyer is looking around. They have a few minutes to get a feel for the home. That is why it is so essential to have a welcoming entryway.

Sprucing up the outside of your door will make your home look warm and inviting from the street. Inside, do not put anything behind your door and keep it in good condition because you want it to open easily and freely.

PROFESSIONAL BONUS TIP:

Have the buyers go through the door with the best viewpoint. For instance, do not put the lockbox on the back door if what they will see are the garbage cans and hose. Typically, the best viewpoint comes from the front door.

Giving Your House a Facelift

> ### PROFESSIONAL BONUS TIP:
>
> The front of the house changes the frame of mind of the seller before they ever enter your home.

When it comes to the exterior of the house, the big decision is whether to paint. When you look at your house from across the street, does it look tired and faded? Is it cracking, peeling, or chipping? Does it compete with the entryway for attention?

If it is, a fresh coat for your exterior may cost you a bit of time and money but may elevate your home from "fixer-upper" to "move-in condition." Paint is often a good investment and really spruces up the appearance of a house, adding dollars to offers from potential home buyers.

> ### PROFESSIONAL BONUS TIP:
>
> Even if you cannot afford to paint your whole house, at least paint the front to give it curb appeal.

When choosing a color, it should not be something showy and unusual, but a color that fits well in your neighborhood. Of course, the color also depends on the style of your house.

> ### PROFESSIONAL BONUS TIP:
>
> Take a picture of your house and print it in black and white. Then keep lightening it until you have simply an outline. Use crayons to color the home and see what the different colors can do. If you are technically savvy, scan or take a picture of your house and use Photoshop

> to play around with its appearance. To change the color of your houses paint or the color of its siding, use the paint bucket tool (for tutorials, go to technical support at Adobe.com). People are more satisfied when they can see what it is going to look like. Look at the one you have and then the one that you have drawn. Ask yourself, "Which one would I want to move into?"

As for the roof, if you know your roof leaks, repair it. If you do not repair a leaky roof, you are going to have to disclose it and the buyer will want an entire new roof. If you know your roof leaks and you do not repair it and do not disclose it, look forward to hearing from lawyers.

PROFESSIONAL BONUS TIP:

If your house can accommodate shutters, put them up, but make sure they fit properly.

CASE STUDY

I have no feeling of difference whatsoever about staging modest homes versus expensive homes. Every home requires the same amount of time, effort, and arrangement of furniture or accessories. The only difference is that one house costs more. Sometimes when you have a small home of 1500 square feet or less, and you have to make it seem larger. That can be a challenge, but the same principles apply.

I have found that most home owners do not recognize the need to stand out above and beyond the rest. They see their house as just as good as everyone else's. And that may be true. But when you put your home on the market and compare it to another similar home, yours will need to stand out. If it does not, why would a buyer choose yours?

If your home was built in the '60s and you still have the original blue flowered wallpaper, you may assume that everyone else in the neighborhood still has it, too. But when you put your home on the market that wallpaper simply will not go over in the current era! Newer homes often have to find a way to stand out among older, more settled homes with beautiful landscaping. Spotty grass and a few tiny shrubs will not go over either!

People do not see their house as a product that you have to market and sell. However, selling your home is like packaging. People look at the outside before deciding to come in. Then they look at the inside before deciding to buy, and it is mostly based on looks. It is packaging. You need to wrap up your product, your home, like a beautiful package.

I do not think that most homes need renovations to sell. Renovations imply large expense and time, and people simply do not want to make those kinds of investments in a house they are selling. I do believe, however, that many homes can use improvements. Perhaps it is purchasing new appliances, changing the wall covering, adding chair rail and crown molding, or upgrading tiles. These are smaller things that people are willing and able to handle.

When it comes to repairs, think about the walls first. If you have holes in your walls or can see where old pictures were once hung, then you need to paint. You should also consider getting new carpet. I think the main repairs are those things that jump out at a potential buyer and cause them to focus on the negative.

Empty homes are a bit harder to stage. However, I use the phrase, "more is less," even though the house is empty. The principle still works. Do not try to clutter an empty room. It needs to be warm and inviting, not cold and distant. I believe that something should be done in every room, but you do not have to do everything full scale.

Creating a Heaven on Earth

The front yard

Landscaping may be far more important than you believe. Gone are the days of equi-distance shrubs along the front of the house and a concrete walk leading to the front steps. Gone are the days when two potted plants, one on either side of the front stoop, filled with the flower of the month provide the only color.

According to the National Gardening Association's 2013 market research survey, Americans spent $29.5 billion on their lawns and gardens last year, or $347 per household. If people are spending this kind of money on creating a beautiful yard, then we can safely say that landscaping is a big deal.

> ## PROFESSIONAL BONUS TIP:
>
> Most people know that the kitchen and baths are essential. I believe completely that outside counts cue to curb appeal, so do not forget the landscaping.

The most important part of landscaping, of course, is the front yard. It is what potential buyers see first. After getting the front entryway in order, you should look at the walk from the car to the door. Is the walk a pleasing one, full of color and interest, or is it full of weeds, brown patches, and monotony? If it is the latter, then your front landscaping needs some work.

The way to create interest is to add flowers and plants to add color. You will also need to trim up any weeds along the way, and especially those that are growing in the cracks of the walkway. And if bare patches simply will not grow grass, try adding a natural area that incorporates the bare areas.

PROFESSIONAL BONUS TIP:

Purchase a few shrubs in pots to place in strategic locations. The seller can take these pots with them to their new house.

One piece of landscaping is what is called the hardscape. Hardscapes are the non-living parts of the landscaping such as paving stones, decks, porches, and patios. Paving stones are a way to create an interesting and pleasing walk from the car to the door. Rather than the straight concrete sidewalk, pavers can meander a bit (not too much because you do not want the buyer to feel that the walk to the door is interminable). They also add texture and color, setting the stage for a yard that screams "relax and enjoy yourself."

And do not forget the driveway. You may pull in and out of your driveway two to three times per day. To and from work, to the store, to the gym, then out for a late night bite. This makes your driveway look worn. Be sure to clean your driveway and make any necessary repairs.

The backyard hardscapes

Once you have gotten the front yard in shape, it is time to work on the backyard. The most important areas of the backyard are the patios, decks, and porches. Getting these areas up to date will give the buyers a feeling that they are getting bonus space.

A patio is no longer a square concrete or brick block with some patio furniture and a string of lights. Patios, porches, and decks are being transformed into outdoor rooms meant for relaxation after a hard day of work.

But does adding something like a patio or deck really add value to your home? According to Remodeling magazine, the "2014 Cost vs. Value Report" shows it does! Investing in a deck will give you a 84.7% return on your investment.

Before: The back entrance to this home is cluttered with overgrown bushes and trees and has an unattractive fence.

After: Trees and plants were trimmed and bamboo fencing was erected to hide the unattractive fence and keep plants on the other side of the fence out of view.

If you decide to add a deck or patio to your home, be sure to create a design that is in keeping with your house's style. Also be sure that it is large enough to "do the job." For instance, if you plan to use your gas grill and have meals out on the deck, a 10x12 square will not work. What can you expect to spend on a deck? According to Porch.com, the average deck costs about $8,300. But remember – you will recoup that and more in the sale. Having a charming outdoor space, as long as the interior is up to par, is a bonus that will help your home sell more quickly.

Lawn furniture is a terrific addition to any yard, especially if it is large. A bench, which is one of the most popular types of lawn furniture, could be used and chairs strategically placed could surround a wooden centerpiece coffee table. Swings are equally popular among the nature lover who is content to enjoy all of the beauty that nature has to offer.

Finally, do not neglect any paths or entrances to the back door. Although the buyer will likely not be coming in the back door, they will eventually head out into the backyard and the only way back in will be through the back entrance.

Backyard landscaping

In addition to the hardscape, you must also look at the landscape – the live portions of your yard. This includes grass, shrubs, trees, and flowers. The vast array of plants now available to home owners is amazing. Unless you happen to be a horticulturist, asking the advice of a local nursery will be your best bet.

Is your landscaping at least average for the neighborhood? If it is not, buy a few bushes and plant them. If you have an area for flowers, buy mature colorful flowers and plant them. They add a splash of vibrancy and color, creating a favorable first impression.

PROFESSIONAL BONUS TIP:

Use larger scale plants instead of smaller ones to give the landscaping a punch.

Your lawn should be evenly cut, freshly edged, well watered, and free of brown spots. If there are problems with your lawn, you should take care of them before working on the inside of your home, because certain areas may need to be planted and will need time to mature. The basic steps to a lush green lawn include:

- Fertilizing your lawn repeatedly (but avoid nitrogen compounds higher than 10 percent)
- Start mowing at the tallest setting (about 3 ½ - 4 inches off the ground) to prevent weeds
- Avoid pesticides, insecticides, and fungicides (leave aeration to earthworms)
- Water deeply but infrequently to encourage deep root growth
- Fertilize once a year in the Fall to establish healthy roots for the next growth season (use fertilizer specific to Fall that uses less nitrogen)
- Look for the three numbers listed on your fertilizer bag to determine their percentages (for example, nitrogen, phosphorus and potassium are the three ingredients, so if the bag says 10-6-4, that means you have 10 percent nitrogen, 6 percent phosphorus, and 4 percent potassium.

"Organic fertilizers are the best because the ingredients are slow to break down in the soil and remain low in chemicals and salts that hurt soil microbes. The most popular (but expensive) organic brand is Ringers with a 10-2-6 ratio. The brand Milorganite, with a 6-2-0 ratio is almost as effective for half the price.

Once you have your plants settled into their new homes, you will want to consider mulch. Mulch will make any garden area look fresher and it has an added bonus when you are selling your home – mulch controls weeds naturally. This means that you will not be faced with the daily chore of pulling the weeds out of your garden beds.

PROFESSIONAL BONUS TIP:

Put fake flowers in with the real flowers in the garden to give the gardens more spectacular color.

Cleaning lawn furniture

To keep your lawn furniture polished and ready for buyers to see, there are a few tips that will make the art of cleaning much simpler.

1. Many commercial cleaning products are designed to be used as furniture polish, but some people are not comfortable using harsh cleaners. A good substitute for cleaning your lawn furniture may include a wet rag with anti-bacterial dish washing liquid being applied just before scrubbing. Be sure to rinse the soap away after you are done for a shiny, polished look.

2. Even outside, dirt and dust can be a problem. Rather than leaving your lawn furniture covered in nature's gunk, take a sheet of Bounce to remove any loose products. Dust is attracted to Bounce and will cling to it right away, but this will only work on material that is not stuck to the surface. Once you are through, toss the bounce in the garbage and be on your way.

Cleaning the driveway

Your driveway takes a beating. You may pull in and out of it two or three times a day. And you may have a two or three car household. Road dirt, sand, mud, oil, and grease is brought onto your driveway from your tires. The messier the roads where you work and live, the worse your driveway can get, but save the hose for the lawn. There is a better method of cleaning your driveway: pressure washing.

For a cement driveway, you will need pressure washers producing at least 3000 PSI. To start, you will want to remove all things from the driveway that would be in your way, like your cars. Remove any loose debris, such as litter and children's toys. If there is any grease, oil, or tire marks you may want to get rid of that first. Do this by soaking it up with sawdust or cat litter. Next, you will want to pre-treat the area. Again, for heavy greasy spots, you may want to use a degreaser. You can soak the entire driveway with cleaning solution for about five or ten minutes to allow any grease to break up. Finally, you finish by spraying the area in even strokes. For a reasonable price, Home Depot offers pressure washer rentals, but make sure you rent a washer with the appropriate PSI for your cleaning purposes. If you're not certain, ask a representative at the store.

Staining a deck

Staining your deck will help it to look great, as well as restore its natural oils and protect it from ultraviolet rays and water damage. However, avoid staining the deck in extreme temperatures. Here is how to apply deck stain.

1. Choose a wood stain in your desired color.
2. Thoroughly clean the deck. Use deck cleaner or a pressure washer. Make sure your cleaner is the one designated for the type of wood you are using. For best results use wood bleach to ensure the original pigment of the wood is achieved in preparations. Use extreme care when using a pressure washer the force of the water can cause injury to people and animals. Follow all the rental company's instructions when using this piece of equipment.
3. Let the deck dry completely.
4. Fill a small bucket or rolling pan with the stain.
5. Immerse a brush or long-handled roller into the stain. Absorb only enough stain for a few strokes.
6. Roll or brush the stain onto the deck. Make sure you apply the stain evenly. Use a paintbrush for hard-to-reach places.

7. Wipe excess stain or dark spots with rags. Never leave used rags, brushes, or containers of stain in the direct sun, or they could combust, creating a fire.

8. Let stain set for 24 hours.

Now that we have our home in order, let's shed a little light on the subject.

Entryway TIPS

194. If you have a cute little plaque or shingle with your family name on it, remove it. Even if it is just on the mailbox. You can always put it up again once you move.

195. Get a new plush doormat. This is something else you can take with you once you move.

Exterior House TIPS

196. Flaws on the outside of a home only make buyers wonder what flaws they will find on the interior of the home.

197. Certain homes are considered historical. If your home is in a designated historical area, you will need permission to make any changes to the outside appearance of your home. This is also true if you live in a community with a home owner's association.

198. Different shades of yellow seem to elicit the best response in home buyers, whether it is in the trim or the basic color of the house.

199. When painting the exterior of your home, paint the garage door the same color as the body of the house.

200. Enhance your home's appearance via exterior lighting. Create visual interest by highlighting porches, walkways, and landscaping using a mix of fixtures and techniques.

Plant TIPS

201. Do not buy bulbs or seeds and plant them. They will not mature fast enough to create the desired effect and you certainly do not want a patch of brown earth for home buyers to view.

202. Do not put in trees. Mature trees are expensive, and you will not get back your investment. Also, immature trees do not really add much to the appearance value or the home.

203. When purchasing flowers, shrubs, and trees for your landscaping projects, be sure to buy plants that grow in your area. Consider climate, the amount of sun the plants will receive, and the soil conditions.

204. If you are selling your home during the spring and summer months, choose different varieties of flowers that will bloom throughout the two seasons. The constant color will help create the curb appeal you desire.

205. If you are in a condo or apartment, the exterior landscaping may be out of your hands. Consider the balcony or patio area as your landscaping and use the same tips found here to create a beautiful space.

Cleanliness TIPS

206. Always rake up loose leaves and grass cuttings.

207. For cleaning decks, use hot water, any liquid cleaner you would use to wash clothes and bleach. The bleach removes stains, mildew, and algae. It is the main ingredient in commercial deck wash.

208. If you have swing sets or anything elaborate for your children, it probably makes more sense to remove them than to leave them in place. They take up room, and you want your back yard to appear as spacious as possible, especially in newer homes where the yards are not as large.

Landscaping TIPS

209. You cannot sell it if they cannot see it.

210. When creating a pathway with bricks or pavers, be sure that they are meant to be in the ground. Many bricks are not meant for this purpose and will crack and crumble over time.

211. When using lumber in hardscapes, be sure that the lumber is pressure treated.

212. When using black plastic edging for flowerbeds, use the straight edging rather than the rolled kind. Edging that has been rolled has the tendency to pop back up out of the ground.

213. The most sought after mulch is double-ground pine bark. It has no dyes, repels insects, and lies flatter, thus making it more attractive.

214. Regrade your landscape away from the house if you have had leakage problems.

215. Asphalt driveways can be seal coated to give it a dark, well-maintained look.

216. The back yard should be tidy. If you have a pool or spa, keep it freshly maintained and cleaned. If you have a dog, be sure to keep the area clear of "debris."

217. Keep flowers blooming and looking good by removing the old blooms. This is a process called "deadheading."

218. If you have a fence or erect one, be sure that it is one your property line and does not encroach into a neighbor's yard.

Chapter 8

Shed Some Light on the Matter

ighting serves many functions, not the least of which is beauty, and beauty translates into money in your pocket as your home increases in value. If you truly want your home to shine, then adding the appropriate lighting will create a warm and inviting atmosphere.

This is easy to say and harder to do. Why? Have you ever checked out the hardware lighting section? If so, you have certainly noticed that the choices are endless, leaving you with the nagging questions of "Which is best and where is it?"

Showing Your Home In Its Best Light

Interior lighting is an art form. It is not just a matter of what fixture you happen to like. Determining the best lighting means analyzing fixture selection plus:

- Fixture placement
- Proper installation procedures
- The art of lighting levels, elements, form, balance, transitions, and texture.

The five most common lighting mistakes are:

1. Using too much lighting
2. Having all the light fixtures clearly visible to the eyes
3. Using high wattage bulbs
4. Creating an "airport runway" effect by setting up all the lights in a straight path
5. Using yellow lights for ambiance instead of blue-white bulbs

Any one of these mistakes will detract from your home, thus making it less desirable for home buyers.

PROFESSIONAL BONUS TIP:

Be sure that all rooms and hallways are well lit   dark rooms are dismal. Change bulb type or wattage if necessary, but be sure that a buyer can see the property.

Enhancing the Beauty

When designing a lighting plan for the rooms in your home, you need to consider the variety of activities that occur there.

If the area is for reading or sewing, you need "task lighting" that allows you to complete your task without being blinded, but without straining your eyes to get the job done! For instance, reading requires task lighting that comes from behind the reader's shoulder or reflects off the ceiling or wall.

Beyond performing tasks, you will also want to highlight or feature certain areas with the use of "accent lighting." When you look around your home, what do you see? More importantly, what do you WANT to see? It may be a particular piece of artwork, an unusual plant, or an interesting architectural feature. For instance, if you have a fireplace made of brick, you may decide to emphasize this feature with recessed lights installed in the ceiling over the mantle. This type of lighting creates an interesting effect across the surface of the stone. No matter what you choose to emphasize, accent lighting will help it stand out and add a dramatic touch.

Finally, there is the "ambient lighting." This is the general lighting that provides overall illumination to the areas in use. Once again, consider the fireplace. Another way to attract attention to this area is by adding wall sconces on each side. Not only does this draw attention to its beauty, but it also adds general lighting to the room.

PROFESSIONAL BONUS TIP:

Lights against the wall are a great way to infuse light throughout the room.

Following are a few general guidelines when incorporating the lighting into your room.

- Lamps that are used for tasks should be approximately 28 inches to 32 inches tall. If a task light is a floor lamp, the best height is at least 40 inches to 42 inches from the floor. Place the light so that it is behind the reader's shoulder with the shade slightly below the reader's nose.
- Avoid placing a lamp in the middle of a table. It should sit forward and closer to the reader.
- For lamps placed on dressers, a good height is 20 inches to 24 inches.
- When selecting a chandelier, you want to pick one that is in good scale to the table. A good rule of thumb is one half of the width of the table plus nine inches.

PROFESSIONAL BONUS TIP:

I always put in the sofa and loveseats and then the tables and lamps. Then I step back and look for the triangle of lighting. If it is there, I know that my furniture placement is correct, for instance, an end table lamp, a floor lamp, and a canned light at the mantel. That is a triangle. I like my triangle of light to come from differing heights as well. This creates drama!

Here Comes the Sun

Another way to "create" light is to let the natural light of the outside in. This can be as easy as washing the windows and opening the blinds. Natural lighting gives a room a warm and spacious feeling and it does not cost a thing.

PROFESSIONAL BONUS TIP:

Open your windows as much as possible. If the windows are ugly, use vertical blinds and keep them open as much as possible.

Another thing to consider is new window treatments. Many older style curtains and draperies were heavy. They were meant for privacy so they blocked out everything on the outside – including light.

New window treatments can make a world of difference. They can add value and style to your home and be something the buyers view as a bonus – something they will not have to buy or replace when they move in. The caution, however, is that you keep the treatments neutral (keep your personality out of the room) and that you make sure they do not block the amount of light that comes into a room.

PROFESSIONAL BONUS TIP:

Many homes have the louvers of the blinds turned down to face the floor. A more enhancing way to use blinds is to turn the louvers up to reflect much-needed ambient light onto the ceiling.

Another simple way to get natural light is to remove the screens from your windows. Not only do screens stop light from entering into your home, they also stop the buyer from being able to see out. This feeling of darkness and confinement is not something you want your buyers to have.

Do you still feel that you need more natural light? Another option to consider is adding a skylight. Skylights now come in all shapes and sizes, as well as a myriad of different materials. And, unlike the skylights of yesteryear, if installed properly, they do not leak.

CASE STUDY

CLASSIFIED CASE STUDIES
™
directly from the experts

No matter whether you are selling a condo, an apartment, a town home, a small house, or a large mansion, staging works as long as it is applied properly. By properly, I mean putting the right props into the right spaces. For instance, I avoid using overly decorated and expensive props in small cottages or condos. The space needs to shine and the architecture needs to pop - not the staging accessories. Sometimes that is best accomplished by less rather than more, even in expensive homes.

When the goal is to accentuate the architecture, the rules apply to all spaces. These rules include getting the furniture into right place in the room, using and adding light correctly, and eliminating the clutter. In fact, it is far more important to get the furniture into the right place in the room than it is to get the right furniture into the room.

No space needs clutter or an overabundance of knickknacks. I focus on installing appropriately sized, colored, and shaped furniture or accessories in the following areas: entryway, living room, dining room, kitchen, master bedroom and bath. Those items may be as simple as hand towels or as elaborate as a leather loveseat with sofa table, lighting, and plants.

Empty spaces will tell you whether they need a lot or a little attention to sell their attributes. For instance, if an empty room leaves little to the imagination about how it is to be used or how to position furniture in it, minimum or no staging is necessary. I can use something as simple as a potted tree placed diagonally across from the entry in the space to help the eye gauge the proportions of the room.

If, however, the space begs to be explained because of unusual angles or architecture, a piece of upholstery or table with chairs may be called for to best showcase its attributes. Remember, an empty room frequently looks smaller than if it is filled with furniture.

I will always do what can be done first to stage the property without renovations because it is my goal to prep the house with as little cost to the seller as possible and save them money. Of course, renovations may be a necessity, but many times simply moving the furniture into the proper alignment to enhance the natural geometry of the architecture will eliminate the need to renovate. For instance, instead of replacing a turquoise asphalt kitchen floor, considered a detriment by many buyers viewing the space, I featured it by adding strategically located turquoise decorative accessories – voila, instant harmony instead of handicap.

Staging works because it leads to quicker sales and more money for the home owner. It is not unusual to hear, "Wow! My socks are knocked off!"

Make It Natural with Man Made Lighting

If you just cannot seem to get enough natural light, you should consider indirect light. Rather than shining outward, indirect light shines upward and reflects off the ceiling to give a natural feeling. This effect is usually created with the addition of sconces in any room of the house.

Recessed lighting is another way to create a natural feeling light. Recessed lighting is installed above the ceiling where only one opening of the light shows. Recessed downlights are the most popular form because they blend into almost any décor and provide a range of lighting effects. Different varieties of recessed lighting can provide ambient, accent, task, and flood lighting depending on their bulbs, housing, and trim.

Home owners should choose recessed lighting when they want something sleek, functional, and affordable that does not call too much attention to itself. This option is all but invisible since the fixture, light bulb, and wiring are all hidden away inside the ceiling, and it turns on via a wall switch. All a buyer will see are the glowing discs of light directed at a countertop, painting, table, or shelving. Once used only under cabinets in the kitchen, recessed lighting has emerged in bathrooms, living rooms, dining rooms, and even bedrooms.

Kitchens are a great place to add recessed lighting to work as a secondary light source with another fixture. Recessed lights can add just the right amount of added light you need while reading recipes or chopping ingredients. They are also a good way to keep a kitchen lit when the main light source is turned off.

The dining room is another room where recessed lights are great as secondary lighting sources. Most people opt for a formal light fixture in their dining room to make the look a dramatic one. Recessed lights are a great way to enhance the overall look and feel of a dining room by adding just the right amount of lighting effect.

The breakfast nook is a wonderful area where recessed lighting can work alone. Most breakfast nooks are right off the kitchen and adding another hanging light fixture can make for an unbalanced look. That is where recessed lighting comes in. They provide a wonderful amount of light over a kitchen table whether you are eating, paying bills, or doing paperwork.

Generally in both bedrooms and living rooms people have ceiling fans installed. Ceiling fans can come with a light kit or without. When used as a secondary light fixture in either a bedroom or living area recessed lighting offers the option for lower light when you are watching TV or just enjoying a cozy evening.

Typically in most bathrooms there are vanity lights above the sink and mirror. In larger bathrooms these vanity lights might not put out enough light to give you adequate lighting while in the shower or tub. Recessed lighting is a wonderful option in that case. It can be used along with the vanity lights or alone.

They Are Not All Made Alike

Sometimes, refreshing a room can be as easy as changing a light bulb. Bulbs like GE Reveal filter out yellow rays common in ordinary light bulbs, making colors, fabric, walls, and artwork appear richer, crisper, and more vivid. Different types of rooms may call for different types of lighting. For example, if you stage a child's room, you want to avoid creating a dramatic effect because shadows scare kids, so you would want to space the lighting evenly with omni-directional Light Emitting Diodes (LEDs). Since the master bedroom is the most important bedroom to stage, you want dramatic lighting to enhance its features, so you might rely on chandelier lighting. Dining rooms would require dimmable LED lighting for entertainment purposes and to create an intimate setting. A living room also requires multiple lighting options (accented and recessed), which makes LED reflector bulbs, such as PARs and MR16s ideal. Bathrooms should have color temperature ranges in the bright-white to daylight range for color accuracy and clarity. Kitchens require warmer lighting tones (reds, oranges, yellows, browns). For lighting tips and products, go to: **www.gelighting.com/LightingWeb/na/consumer/moodcam.jsp**

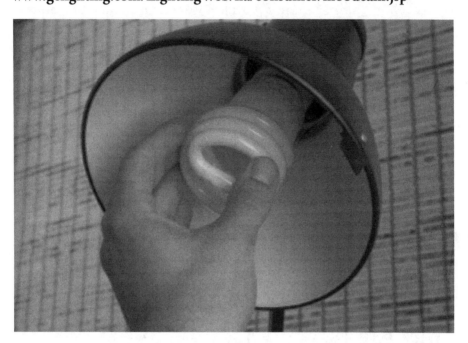

PROFESSIONAL BONUS TIP:

Since you need to leave the lights on when showing your house, considering using daylight bulbs. This is the best transition from the daylight outside to your home inside. It keeps your buyer from going from bright sun to dark interior.

It is amazing the impact lighting has in our homes and in our lives. A 2013 survey by Home Goods found that 46 percent of Americans felt better lighting alone could improve their mood, as well as negative feelings about their living space. To determine what mood you've created from your home's lighting, go around your house and check to see how the lighting reflects the mood you intend for the different rooms. .

A Look at Living and Lighting

Kitchen

Earlier I discussed the use of recessed lights in the kitchen to provide task lighting when cooking. However, recessed lights are not the only options for creating a warm but bright atmosphere.

One fixture that will add drama to your kitchen is a pendant light. This is a ceiling mounted light hanging on a chain from the ceiling. Typically a pendant light is used over a kitchen table or an island.

Bathroom

According to the American Lighting Association, the follow seven tips are a great way to light up your bathroom:

- Light the shower so that it is bright enough to make shaving easier.
- Installing linear lights in the toe space below the vanities is a great way to provide a night-light.
- Cove lighting adds a soft warm glow
- Vertical wall sconces on either side of the mirror are an excellent way to provide even facial lighting needed for applying makeup.
- Table lamps add a nice touch to bathrooms as long as they are displayed away from water sources.
- Adding a decorative light fixture suspended from the ceiling makes adds an elegant touch to any bathroom.
- A focused light over the commode makes for good reading.

Front entrance

Make your entry area well lit, both inside and out. That said, on the inside, do not settle for the standard, garish overhead light. Put some thought into attractive lighting fixtures, which are generally easy to update. Use decorative fixtures, shades, or tinted light bulbs to ensure that everyone looks fabulous when they step into your house.

Basement

Basements, even daylight basements, are known to be dark and dreary. Since this is true, you need to be sure not to skimp on the lighting or the basement will be seen as a liability instead of an asset.

In some cases, you will be able to increase the natural light in the room by increasing the size of the basement windows. The other option is to install a skylight tube.

A skylight tube is a natural lighting option ideal for kitchens, bedrooms, halls, walk-in closets, and yes, basements. There are many innovative designs to meet most house and roof designs.

The basic design concept is a tube, between 10 and 20 inches in diameter, with a highly reflective-interior. The tube runs from the roof to the ceiling. On a sunny day, a skylight tube can provide the equivalent lighting of ten 100-watt light bulbs. From indoors, it looks just like a bright globe light fixture on the ceiling.

The top of the tube, which extends through the ceiling, is covered with a waterproof clear acrylic plastic dome. The dome shape captures sunlight and is naturally cleaned whenever it rains. It extends only a few inches above the roof. An optional reflector can increase the brightness. Complete do-it-yourself installation should take about two hours.

If the attic space above the area where you need light has obstructions, choose a skylight tube made of flexible corrugated material. This special material is reflective on the inside and can be bent and twisted in any direction.

Skylight tubes are much more efficient than standard skylights because they have so much less surface area. The long, sealed tube, which is filled with air, forms an insulating column from the roof to the ceiling. When installed properly, there is no air leakage.

Lighting TIPS

219. Most rooms can use more lighting.
220. No matter what you choose to emphasize, accent lighting will help it stand out and add a dramatic touch.
221. Every average sized room should have a minimum of 3 sources of lighting. So when you plan your lighting, you want to think of the place as a giant triangle. Try to put a lamp at every point of the triangle and you will find it pretty easy to balance the room with light.
222. When trying to achieve the right balance of ambient lighting, place lighting so that every 50 square feet has the same amount of light as produced by a 100-watt bulb.
223. In small spaces, light helps to visually expand the room. Lights under cabinets can also give the illusion of more countertop space.
224. To make ceiling fans feel more up-to-date, replace old globes with new ones.

225. Large framed mirrors can reflect light from lighting fixtures as well as windows, thus making the room feel even lighter and airier. Adding a mirror has the added bonus of making the room appear to be larger.

226. Up lights cast interesting shadows drawing the eye upward, increasing the appearance of a larger space while giving a touch of drama.

227. Get rid of your sheers. They will make your home look dated and dark.

228. Take a look at your bathroom lighting. If it has a strip full of light bulbs over the mirror, replace it. This type of fixture is extremely outdated and creates an unusual glow.

229. Do not forget the glow of candles. Candles can be a great way to create accent lighting.

230. When using different sources of lights in your kitchen, be sure to coordinate the types of bulbs you use. You want the tone of your floor, counters, and cabinets to look the same in all part of the room.

231. Wire lights separately so that you can create zones of light. This way, you can light up certain areas while not lighting up others.

232. Ceiling mounted light boxes are unattractive and can cast unnatural shadows.

233. Place a vase or sculpture by a window that gets plenty of natural light. Doing so will highlight this area.

234. Three-way bulbs give you reading and working light when you need it and the cozy ambience of lower wattage when you do not.

Chapter 9

Staging on a Shoestring

What is Budget Staging?

The term "staging" is easy to understand; it concerns making something (a room, a space) prettier, better organized, more functional, and more esthetically pleasing. The budget part comes in when you have limited amount to spend on the staging process.

You may have a zero dollar budget, but you can still re-arrange your space, clean and de-clutter it, and look around your house for items to use in new, more effective, or unusual ways. You can create a pleasant, comfortable area without breaking the bank.

Budget staging is really about getting the most value and impact for whatever dollars you have available to spend. It involves some stretching of the imagination to see the potential in less expensive accessories and furniture.

It is important to spend your money on the most important items first. If you are staging a bedroom, make sure that you have a bed. If it is a home office that you feel the need to spiff up, think about the desk and the desk chair.

Alternative Methods to Big Money

Look for alternatives to everything!!! Flat sheets on sale are a great buy. I can get one at my discount store for $2.89. A flat sheet is generally 66x96 inches; that is over three yards of fabric for less than 97 cents a yard! You cannot beat the price or the selection since flat sheets come in so many colors. Use them for table covers, curtain panels, making comforter covers, throw pillow covers, or even casual slipcovers!

> ☝ **PROFESSIONAL BONUS TIP:**
>
> Before buying a new comforter, consider flipping over the one you have. Put the plain side up.

Look for furniture at yard sales and in the classifieds. You can get quality furniture this way for a fraction of what it would cost you new.

Finally, look for good resources to help you learn to create your own accessories, custom paint finishes, and inspirational ideas.

You do not have to spend a large sum of money to get a large sum of money in your pocket at closing.

This Could Be You:
A Real Estate Agent Success Story

An older couple was moving into an assisted living facility and had their home on the market for 6 months. They were on a fixed income and now had to pay two mortgages. They decided to switch Realtors and bring in a Realtor that I work with frequently. The Realtor brought me in to evaluate the property. I saw that the home owner's personal taste was overwhelming the space. I recommended removing the outdated wallpaper and painting the rooms a more neutral color. In the second bedroom, the home owner had added a built in desk that took up 3 of the 4 walls. They were selling the space, not the huge computer desk. The desk was not allowing buyers to know the purpose of the space. I brought in my own furniture and accessories for this room to show prospective buyers how best use the space. The home went back on the market and they had a full price offer in one day! Amazing what staging can do!

Creating a Classy Kitchen

Regardless of your budget, you have to create a kitchen worth viewing. If the curb appeal has gotten them in the door, the kitchen will keep them there. So, what are some low budget options to create a high budget effect?

Flooring makes a huge difference in the appearance of a kitchen or bath. If vinyl flooring is dated and worn, you can lay new vinyl or laminated wood material right over the old flooring. Many of the items available today give the look of ceramic tile or natural wood at a lower cost.

Faux granite countertop

Next in line are the countertops. You can create the look of stone counters for less than $40! The secret? Paint. Get a book from the library, or search the Internet for instructions on the stone faux finish of your choice, then follow these steps.

1. For this to be successful, there is one step you cannot skimp on. Prime your countertops with a primer specially made for non-porous surfaces!!! Bin or KILZ are both good brands.
2. Now paint your faux finish.
3. Allow to dry thoroughly, 24 hours is best.

4. Now simply give it 4 or 5 coats of water-based polyurethane, let dry, and enjoy years of a beautiful kitchen!

5. Save some of your original paint so if you ever do get a chip, touch up is a breeze.

I promise you, buyers will be hard pressed to tell that it is not a $5,000 counter!

Lighting is another way to add flair to your kitchen. For an easy and inexpensive way to brighten up a kitchen, install under-the-counter lighting. A small purchase at the hardware store is all it takes to completely change the way the light hits the surfaces of a room.

Then there is the molding. You read earlier how fancy molding can really update a kitchen. But have you priced molding? Anything beyond the basic is beyond the budget conscious seller. That is why I suggest that you make your own.

You can make carved look molding for little money. You can either use joint compound and a cake-decorating bag to create beautiful designs on plain wood strips, then prime and paint, or use a "salt dough" method.

To use the dough method, mix up a batch of salt dough like the kind that children often use for making Christmas decorations. To make the molding, simply cut the dough into uncomplicated shapes such as leaves, ropes, or scrolls. Then let dry or bake as the recipe dictates. Now use a glue gun to attach to wood strips, prime, and paint! Adding fancy molding is a great way to create a rich looking kitchen.

Sometimes "shoestring staging" is as simple as placing the furniture differently in the room. Placing furniture at an angle can do wonders as you can see from the photos on the following page. What was once a typical dining room now looks elegant with nothing more than the removal of a hutch, a change of a centerpiece, the addition of a plant, and the angle of the table and chairs.

This Could Be You: **TAKE A LOOK!**

Before

Notice that the table is now at an angle giving this room a more dramatic flair.

If you have a round table that cannot be angled, you can angle the chairs for the same effect.

Is Your Bathroom Boring?
Make Your Bathroom Bold

As you know, bathrooms are an important part of staging because they are an important part of the sale. But what if you just do not have the money to put in new counters or flooring? Here are a few simple things you can do to add the decorator's touch without spending a fortune.

Search the house for accessories to use in your bathroom. Roll up hand towels in a wine rack. Use a pretty mug for cosmetic brushes or cotton swabs. Stand a picture on the counter in a metal plate holder. Choose a pretty candy dish in place of a plastic soap dish. A crystal or metal tray can serve to keep perfume bottles together. Any such containers can help you camouflage those items that simply have to be kept in the bathroom. However, by adding something unique, you jazz up the space.

Next you want to consider the fabric found in a bathroom. Either a bold, colorful floral print or simple check or stripe can add color to windows or showers. You can purchase or make a shower curtain or window valance to put color around the room. Cording or coordinating accents add a decorator touch.

And then there is art. Most bathrooms have at least one bare wall with no fixtures. What a great place to hang a single piece or collection of framed prints. You do not need to invest a lot of money. Use postcards from travels, lovely pressed flowers, or mementos of travels or hobbies.

Bedroom Bliss on a Budget

How do you go about creating a cozy bedroom on a budget? The first thing you can do is move the furniture. Something this simple can make a huge difference in how it feels. This is one of the easiest ways I know of to make a room feel new... and it does not cost a dime.

You can also consider buying a new comforter or bedspread with matching sheets. These sets can be found at local outlets for a small sum. If you are not able to buy an entire set, then get just one or two items. The bed covering and pillow shams make the largest difference, so I would suggest starting with those.

The most delightful accent is to make generous use of decorative pillows. Pile your bed high with them using a variety of sizes and styles, colors and patterns. Layered pillows give a lush feel to any bedroom.

Keep in mind that the goal of your bedroom design idea is to calm and soothe. So, choose fabrics that are soft and cozy. Select silks, cottons, and suedes. Even terry cloth can add an unexpected luxury.

CASE STUDY

The fundamental difference is that I redesign the home for a whole new look in just a matter of hours using the buyer's items. At the evaluation, it is my job to convince the seller to repaint and remove. You tell them when they have too much stuff or too much furniture. If the client has a pool table in the dining room and either will not take it out or cannot take it out, then I work with that. I simply turn the dining room into the pool hall! That is what a good redesigner will do. We always work with what our clients have.

There is a need to depersonalize the space, as far as getting rid of a lot of the photos, but as a redesigner I think that each room needs to be personalized. People cannot visualize. They cannot see what is not there. That is why I give each room some sense of purpose.

The biggest issue home owners face is wrapping their brain around the concept that their house is no longer a home but a product. People are so emotionally involved in their home that they have trouble turning that off. It is like a box of cereal on the shelf. Why does someone grab Cheerios rather than Rice Krispies? It often comes down to the box!

You have to remember that the person buying your home does not want your memories. They want to create their own. You help them do that by getting rid of your memories. You have got to pack anyway; you may as well start now!

Many people are under the impression that staging only works on larger, more expensive homes. Nothing could be further from the truth. I believe that more modest homes need staging even more than large homes.

The home price does not make as much impact as the condition of the furnishings and the building itself. The same problems can exist in both expensive and modest homes. It is not about price but condition. The person who lives in a more expensive area will have more money to spend. Those staging modest homes will need to be more creative and clever with what they have to work with. The challenge can be different, but the task remains the same!

The problem with the idea that modest homes need staging is that the home owners often do not want to spend money to repair the home properly. They see that they are moving, and they just want to sell their home as is. They do not realize that "as is" will not sell quickly or for more money. They do not realize that by not investing a bit of time, elbow grease, and a few dollars, they can get out of that house quickly!

I often give minor renovation advice like replacing a cabinet and sink in the bathroom, painting kitchen cabinets, changing kitchen hardware, putting in new carpet, painting, or replacing countertops. Huge renovations do not work because the seller is moving. If they wanted to renovate, they would have already done so and would probably be staying. That is why I think that smaller ideas work and make a world of difference.

When I suggest any renovations, I always talk about kitchens and baths. Then I talk about front walkways, doors, and entries. Always consider putting up a new porch fixture or doorknob. Brush down the cobwebs in the eaves. Do not overlook the obvious!

Finally, do not forget the props. These are the smaller items that give the room a finished look. Towels, bedding, potted plants, and artwork are among the items I suggest purchasing. But be sure to buy for your next house. For instance, if you are moving to Palm Springs, consider buying a potted palm rather than a fica tree and take it with you when you go. Do the same thing with the towels. If you do not know the color of your new bath, then buy something neutral.

When you think of landscaping, there are two kinds of overkill. You do not want buyers to have to beat their way through your jungle or step around an abundance of lawn decorations. You also do not want them to walk up a barren wasteland that looks unappealing and uninviting.

You have to remember the curb appeal thing. The front entry is the first impression. You have to get them in the front door. Forgetting curb appeal will not let that happen.

I believe that home stagers or redesigners need to work together as a team with real estate agents and home sellers. Each person on the team has a job to do and these jobs need to be done according to a timeline to get the home sold quickly.

The agent's job is to market. The home owner's job is to prep the property. The stager's job is to give it the model home look. We each have a job. If one does not do the job properly, it wreaks havoc for the others on the team. I find that educating the home owner and the agent that we are a team and that we have to create a timeline and work it together helps everyone get their jobs done on time.

Pictures for the Poor

Ah, artwork the ornaments of the wealthy. Or are they? You do not have to buy expensive art or frames to get an expensive look.

To find frames, look at garage sales and thrift shops   even if the picture inside is hideous, the frame itself might be well worth the measly buck you paid for it.

Once you have a frame, though, what do you put inside? As you know, large prints cost big bucks. Even small prints can get costly. This is where you have to use a bit of imagination.

Try cutting out photos from garden catalogs and frame them for great looking botanical photos. You can do the same using old calendar photos, bookplates, and greeting cards. These can often be found at end of the year clearance sales, used bookstores, and even garage sales.

And finally, do not limit yourself to pictures. Visit your local antique stores and search for inexpensive collectibles that you can group together on a wall. Utensils, postcards, and old keys, can offer a graphic and creative display, and can be inexpensive!

This Could Be You:
A Real Estate Agent Success Story

A former real estate broker attempted to sell her high-end river-view home for six months before allowing me to stage it using her own furnishings. It then sold within twenty-four hours, at the first showing. She even sold her sofa!

Furniture Makeovers

Furniture can be a big problem because good furniture is too expensive and cheap furniture is…well…cheap. When you are trying to sell your home, you definitely do not want it to come across as cheap. If it does, you will get lowball bids because the buyer believes the house is not worth as much.

So, if you cannot afford new furniture, consider making it over. Let's start with basic makeovers for upholstered furniture.

The most well known makeover for an upholstered piece is the slipcover. One large piece of fabric, strategically placed and tucked, can transform a sofa or chair, and change the entire feel of a room.

Here are instructions for some simple, casual covers that almost anyone can do.

First of all, use sheets instead of pieced fabric; it is MUCH easier and cheaper! Measure your furniture, and buy a sheet size that will cover your furniture piece without its cushions, tucked in and around the arms. Do not forget to check out garage sales for good deals. Use decorative cording, if you like, to tie around the "skirt" area to give it a more structured look. Then, simply tuck the ends of the fabric under the couch or chair. You could even tape or staple the ends to the bottom of the piece.

Now it is time to cover the cushions. Take each of your cushions and look at it as if you are wrapping a gift. Cut a piece of material large enough for your cushion, wrap it like a present, and safety pin it to the underside of the cushion. Add a few pillows and a throw, and you have changed the entire look of your furniture for little money. The best part is that the covers are washable.

Sheets, blankets, and quilts can all be used for this project, and can be found at garage sales, thrift stores, and maybe even your own linen closet.

Even dining room chairs can be slip-covered. Simply make an open envelope of fabric to fit over the back of the chair, similar to a pillowcase. If you like, this can be dressed up by tying it with cord or ribbon, sewing on decorative buttons, or adding a little lace. This project can easily be made from leftover curtain fabric and scraps lying around your sewing room.

Next on the list is what is known as "hard goods." Tables, chests, and entertainment centers all fit this category.

Bookcase before painting

A fast and inexpensive way to transform these items is, you guessed it, paint. Almost anything can be painted these days, including laminate. Simply prime it with a product specifically made for non-porous surfaces like BIN or KILZ, then use ordinary house paint.

Budget staging is doable. It just takes a bit of imagination, ingenuity, and effort.

Bookcase after painting

Budget Staging TIPS

235. Move natural light further into rooms by bouncing it off the ceiling. A window located close to the ceiling works for this, as do louvers or operable blinds that can help direct light.

236. Borrow furniture and accessories from friends and family. Old furnishings give your house and old look. Borrowing newer items is a great way to jazz up your house with no expense.

237. Learn to make do with the furniture you have with the art of disguise. Slipcovers, paint, and floor length tablecloths go a long way toward dressing up an otherwise forgettable piece of furniture.

238. If your towels are acceptable, add trim to spruce them up with a decorator look. Simple ribbon banding above the border is a great touch. Be sure to wash the ribbon banding before sewing it on the towels, as it might shrink with the first wash.

239. Bring in extra color buy adding colorful hand towels or washcloths as accents.

240. Dress up that large frameless mirror. Hang swags of fabric from cup hooks to hide and soften the edges of the mirror, and to give it a "frame."

241. Practice faux finish techniques on cardboard before starting in on walls, floors, or counters.

242. Try putting your bed in a corner instead of against a wall. This gives the room a more homey, intimate, and elegant touch.

243. Something as simple as a bowl (or interesting container) of oranges can create an interesting touch to any room.

244. Bring the mirrored dresser from the bedroom and use it for a side table in the living room or use a chest of drawers to hold towels and sundries in the bathroom.

245. An unused bedspread is big enough to make a complete slip cover. If you do not have one, a second hand store is sure to,

and at a much more frugal price than furniture 'throws', which are the same thing large pieces of material.

246. Forget the square corners put a chair or couch or bookshelf at an angle (caddy corner). It rearranges space completely.

247. Break out of the square mold. Think triangle, think circle, think rectangle. Arrange seating in those shapes.

248. Hide inexpensive lighting behind a sofa or plant to add major drama.

249. Add a vase and fresh flowers for an inviting touch.

250. Use local and online resources like www.craigslist.org and **www.freecycle.org** to find free or inexpensive furniture, lamps, and accessories.

251. Spend your money where you can see it. Spending a large sum on a small vase is not nearly as effective as spending it on bold artwork or classic furniture.

252. Distract the eye from what you cannot afford to change by attracting attention with something else that is bright and bold.

253. Bring nature inside. If you do not have a green thumb, silk plants and trees will do the trick as well.

254. Replace your cabinet hardware with new pulls and knobs. Plenty of styles are available to help modernize the look of your kitchen.

255. Though it might seem strange to pull out your Christmas lights in the middle of the summer, wrapping that small iridescent string of white bulbs around tree trunks and branches will bring a romantic, starry atmosphere to your backyard.

256. Do not be afraid to use old indoor chairs outside -- especially if they are just taking up space in the garage. Change their look and get them ready for summer by recovering cushions with colorful fabric.

257. Bed skirts make most beds look soft and sophisticated and are an inexpensive decorating investment. They come in a variety

of patterns, colors, and textures. Soft and neutral in color is the most versatile and pretty. You do not want it to be a focal point, but you do want it be the finishing touch on a bed.

258. A swag at the top of the window is inexpensive and not too dramatic.

259. Hang a curtain rod and simply fold fabric placemats or napkins over it. If they are square, hang them on the diagonal. For rectangular fabric, fold lengthwise. Another option is to fold all of the rectangular fabric the same length, or fold in half on each end, allowing it to drape in the middle.

260. Fronts of dishwashers and some refrigerators are easily replaceable. Most manufacturers offer several colors. Appliance paint can also bring you a new color. Just remove the handles and use masking tape on any areas you do not want painted.

261. A new shower curtain for under $20 with unique shower hooks can make a big difference. If your bathroom is small, using a clear shower curtain or one in the same color as the tub will give the illusion of a bigger bathroom.

Chapter 10

Small Touches for Large Profits

he moment before you open your door to allow the first potential buyer in, there are several things you can do that will add that special touch to your home: the thing that will make your home stand out from all the rest.

This chapter focuses on the final touches that create ambiance. I will provide a series of tips from professionals along with photos so that you can get an idea of what truly attracts a buyer.

This Could Be You:

A Real Estate Agent Success Story

I had one couple that following everything I suggested to the letter. They took off the faded wallpaper in the kitchen. They added some end tables to the living room. They made some adjustments to furniture placement and they removed the items I suggested. They spent a total of $500. Their house sold within 24 hours and they got more than their asking price!

The Right Touch In the Kitchen

Consider staging fresh fruit in the kitchen. Psychology comes into play whenever you are selling your home. Consider buying inexpensive frames from a discount store and print out the words Yum and Good Food on nice paper and hang them in the frames in your kitchen. This gives the subtle feeling of happiness and warmth.

A realtor staging rooms may go through bushels of green apples, pineapples, and coconuts. Pineapples smell so wonderful in the kitchen! Some even put artichokes on the mantel. This can be a way of connecting with the buyer and standing out from the other homes. Whatever is in season is fair game.

The refrigerator is more than just cleaned out – it is staged it with a bottle of wine, grapes, and Brie. Potential buyers would much rather see that then a dirty ketchup bottle and old lunchmeat! A kitchen needs to look used without being cluttered. Consider using a cutting board with fake fruits, breads, and cheese.

Many realtors suggests creating a setting where a party or event is about to happen, such as a buffet dinner or wine tasting. Do not set the table formally, because it is so predictable, and buyers know you are not going to have a dinner party after they leave.

This Could Be You: TAKE A LOOK!

Fresh fruit and a dramatic flair to the table give this kitchen the spark it needs.
Faux fruit is also acceptable as long as it is high quality.

Simple place settings with wine glasses give this kitchen a feeling of elegance.

This Could Be You: TAKE A LOOK!

Before: Eating area before staging. It has no real purpose.

After: Set this way, the room has purpose. The cart gives the room a bit of elegance.

The kitchen is set for a wine tasting, the open cookbook lets you know the kitchen can be used, and the red accessories give the entire room a sense of fun.

Do Not Forget the Dining Room

When setting a table, be sure not to overdo. If you add too much to the table, you will be creating visual clutter. One way to keep clutter to a minimum is to have a nice centerpiece in the middle of the dining room table. Closed curtains makes buyers feel that the neighborhood must be unsafe because you feel the need to keep everything closed up.

The dining room had too much covered up
and the closed curtains gave it a dark look.

With the table at an angle, the curtains opened, and the table
showing, this dining room looks quite inviting.

Relaxing, Romantic Bathrooms

Add pampering accessories! Things like bath bubbles, fluffy towels, and candles not only add the pampering feeling you are trying to achieve, they offer visual comfort with color and texture as well. Psychologically, we all crave that long soak with a good book, and even if we are only in the bathroom for 10 minutes to whip on some make up, just seeing those items displayed promises wonderful baths to come!

PROFESSIONAL BONUS TIP:

People are most sensitive to scent. When creating a beautiful bath, be sure to stick with no scent or low scent candles and soaps.

The Bedroom Retreat

Many realtors know that it is important to have fresh bedding, pillows, and throws. If any of these look tattered, the house will not sell as quickly. Most people, when buying a home, are moving up in the world. You want them to feel that way when they see your home.

Many realtors suggest getting new bedding but warn that you should avoid wild patterned sheets – neutral linens with a few big cushy pillows looks inviting.

The master bedroom is supposed to be the place of refuge for busy adults, but rarely is that way. Instead it is the home to everything that has no home as well as computers and TVs. Make the bedroom a refuge by adding a bistro set and a couple of teacups. This makes the buyer see the bedroom as a place for relaxation where the children will be perfect and all will be lovely.

The master bedroom is important. You should add something that has a dreamy look, like a tray on the bed with a rose and a book, or wine glasses on the bedside table.

This Could Be You: TAKE A LOOK!

This tub says luxury and beckons buyers to imagine themselves soaking in the tub surrounded by glowing candles and soft music.

Adding a tray with grapes and tea, as well as highlighting the fireplace, gives this master bedroom a cozy feeling.

The angle of the bed, along with the pillows and ambient light, makes this bedroom relaxing.

The craziest thing my firm has ever done was to have a piano company loan us a $70,000 piano for a $6 million home to show perspective buyers how the vaulted ceilings in the living room were designed for the best acoustics when playing the piano!!! This is the role of a stager: to show off the best qualities of your home!

I believe that home staging works for all properties regardless of the price point because home staging is about preparing your home for a faster and more profitable sale and marketing your property to the most potential buyers for its target audience. I have staged homes ranging from $100,000 to $10 million and have had the same result- the homes sell faster and for top dollar compared with the competitors within their price range.

I feel that it is important for us to educate the home seller that selling their home means that we are now selling a product. We are not selling their home, their personal taste, their collections, or their treasures and trophies. We are selling the physical space of their home, the structure, and the architectural details. To do so, they need to move out emotionally and divorce themselves from the home.

We are also selling a feeling about the space and that is why they need to stage the home and not simply empty the house so it is vacant- we need to create an atmosphere that allows the buyers to see the potential in the space for them and their family. We can achieve this through selling the maximum space or finding a purpose for every room in the house (is that extra room best shown as a guest room or a home office). This is also achieved through proper furniture placement, uncluttering of personal items, and adding appropriate artwork and accessories.

I feel that as a professional real estate stager, it is my job to prepare the home for a faster and more profitable sale and to give my client a complete plan for this process including our staging recommendations, and any necessary renovations we feel are needed. Rarely do I suggest full remodeling such as redoing the kitchen or bathrooms unless I feel that the price point of the home demands this.

During my consultation, I will educate the home seller about all the necessary things I feel are needed to properly market the home. I tell home owners that when they are selling their homes they cannot control the market conditions or the location of their home, but there are two things they can control- the price of their home and the way buyers perceive it. Staging can change the buyer's perception.

In some cases, simply bringing in furniture, artwork and accessories will not accomplish this. That is when I recommend such things as painting, refinishing floors, updating outdated light fixtures etc. With more expensive homes, I might suggest even further renovations. For example, we had a home owner that wanted $1.75 million for their home with a 15 year old kitchen in a neighborhood where homes were selling for $1.5 million with brand new kitchens. We recommended to the home owner that they consider replacing the countertops with granite, painting the kitchen cabinets a color that was more on trend, and adding new hardware to give the kitchen a mini face lift. For a home that is in a lower price point I would have recommended painting the kitchen cabinets and updating the hardware and light fixtures but not investing in the granite countertops since the home owner would not necessarily recover this investment in the sale. I take the same approach regardless of the price of the home, however my recommendations take into consideration the other homes within the price point of the home I am analyzing. I always consider the price of the home and the competition to make this determination.

I often have to be honest with the home owner that their dollars will be better invested doing minor repairs than having me stage the home around their neglected maintenance issues. I have even recommended that they address some structural things before putting the home on the market like repairing the torn up kitchen floor or replacing the broken seals in the windows in the living room.

Correcting minor maintenance issues such as refinishing the hardwood floors (you are selling the floors not your area rugs!), giving the home a fresh coat of paint where needed, professionally cleaning the carpets and windows, and having a professional cleaning service detail your home makes a difference. It is important to note however, that stagers are not home inspectors or general contractors and some issues are best addressed by these professionals.

My goal first and foremost is to use what the home owner already has in their home. I want them to make an investment of the time and energy preparing the home for sale, not spend their dollars on buying things to redecorate their homes. In some homes however, the home owner's personal taste may be distracting to potential buyers and I may need to enhance their furniture, artwork etc. with pieces that I rent them for a small fee. This is often the case with home owners that have not updated their furniture or accessories for years and now are marketing their homes to younger buyers - think baby boomers downsizing and the younger pottery barn group moving in.

In vacant homes, I recommend adding furniture and accessories to allow the buyer to envision how they will live in the home. It is important to show a purpose for each space and to give perspective to the architectural details in the home. To do so, I rent my own furniture and accessories because it is much less to rent items than to purchase them.

I do not use a checklist with my clients. I believe that stagers that use checklists are not looking at each home as a unique property that needs to be marketed in a unique way. There are things that we address in each home - professionally clean your home, steam clean your carpets, wash your windows, have your lights on and toilet seats down. This however is NOT staging; this is common sense and any stager that charges their client for a checklist and does nothing more is not being a professional stager.

No one can explain the amazing success of staging better than a home owner or a realtor that has experienced the results. One seller told me, "You have totally transformed our listing AND our way of doing real estate. We will never suggest reducing a home's price to the seller without first offering up the opportunity to stage their home to see if we can get the price they want. As you taught us, spending a minimal amount of dollars to stage a home vs. the thousands lost in a sales price reduction is just brilliant! The proof is in the pudding. Our listing was just sitting there, limp and tired. In a single day, after the home owners did their homework from the list you gave them, you came in and breathed life into the wings of this home."

The "before" picture is anything but relaxing.

The "after" photo shows a calm, quiet setting for chess or reading.

Living in the Living Room

The living room needs to have a livable quality. A realtor may suggest putting out a game table with something like Scrabble or chess. In this way, buyers know that the room can be used for family fun and quiet pursuits. It is a dramatic difference from their normal fast paced lives.

Some realtors suggests soft music in the background. When you are staging, it slows the buyer down and puts them in the house. It is subtle but means so much.

Reality Check

✓ An older lady had her home on the market. Somewhere along the line, she got emotionally involved in the sale and called her realtor to say that she could not show her house because she had been struck by lightning. However, the realtor was on the way with potential buyers. She met them in the yard and sprayed them down with a hose!

If at all possible, it is best to leave your home during showings.

The Entryway – The Next Best Thing To Curb Appeal

Consider adorning the entryway with a table, table lamp with a pink light bulb (casts a warm, soft glow), and a mirror over the table, so the buyer "sees himself living there." She also includes a bowl of wrapped candy and a floral arrangement or greenery.

Many realtors will have interesting ideas on items that can be left in the entryway or in the kitchen. If you are in a smaller town that may seem more inaccessible, have a nice paper that welcomes buyers to town. Tell them how many miles it is to the nearest Wal-Mart and where the doctor facilities are located. Give them the flavor of the town. This was done to one of my houses and it sold that day. It allayed the buyer's apprehension about moving to a smaller, out of the way community. If you have a historical house, make a Digital Video Recording (DVR) of the history of the house and send each buyer home with a DVR.

Kitchen and Dining Room TIPS

262. If you have a dining room and a kitchen, set one, but not both.
263. If a table does not look good, cover it with a tablecloth.
264. Always set the table. This includes adding a simple centerpiece, flatware, napkins, and a nice set of dinnerware.
265. Fruit is appealing – try to use fresh or natural looking reproduction wherever possible.
266. Serve cookies, coffee, and soft drinks. It creates a welcoming touch. But be sure the kitchen has been cleaned up; use disposable cups so the sink does not fill up.

Bathroom TIPS

267. For a powder room or extra bath that does not get a hard workout, elegant silk accents on walls and light fixtures create an exotic, luxurious feeling at a small expense.
268. Candleholders with colored candles and pretty vases with flowers or greens will make the bathroom feel more attractive.
269. Always get new towels for the bathroom. Not just clean used, but brand new. You might even consider learning a little fancy folding and adding some fancy soaps.
270. If you have room in your bathroom, bring in a chair and cover with fabric. It makes the room feel more a room, instead of just a utilitarian space.

271. Light candles in the bathroom.

272. Get some cheap strawberry bath bubbles at the drug store, and run a half tub full of hot water with the bubbles. After you let the water out, the room will have a pleasing atmosphere, and most people will not know why.

Living Area TIPS

273. Always leave key light on, even during daylight hours, to create drama. These lights might be in the foyer or over the mantel. Leaving these lights on will draw the buyer's eye to these features. You are helping the buyer know where to look.

274. For rooms that you want to have a warm, cozy feeling, use softer lights.

275. Keep quiet music playing. Easy listening is a good choice.

276. Never have the television on when showing your house.

277. Think about your candles or potpourri. It may smell good to you, but not to everybody! Ninety percent of Americans prefer the smell of pumpkin pie over any other. You might want to invest in some pumpkin pie candles to light during showings!

278. Check the thermostat to make sure that the house is at a comfortable temperature.

279. Consider a guest registration book for visitors to sign.

280. Pets should be kept away from open house visitors. It may be a good idea to have a friend or family member takes care of your pets until the showing is over.

281. If your home does not have plants, you may want to buy a few before the showing. Plants can provide a warm feel and help make buyers feel more at home.

Bedroom TIPS

282. On the night stand, have a spate of new magazines along with a water glass and a decorative bowl filled with candy.
283. Bring in vases of fresh flowers and bowls of fresh fruit.
284. Add fresh logs to the fireplace.

Storage Areas and Outdoor TIPS

285. It pays to have a few stacked boxes to the side of the basement. It sends a marketing message that you are getting ready to move and that you are motivated.
286. Turn on the sprinklers for 30 minutes to make the lawn sparkle.
287. During warm weather, opening windows to let in a breeze is a nice touch.
288. Invite visitors into your home by placing yellow flowers near or at the entry porch. Yellow draws the eye, and potential buyers will feel immediately welcome.

Sample Staging...

Chapter 11

Living In a Home For Sale

ut we have to live here! Yes you live there, but the closer you get to the ideal of the "model" home, the better off you will be. These temporary inconveniences will really pay off in increased offers.

Just think of that great vacation spot you go to or that nice hotel suite you stayed in. They are designed to be just relaxing, uncluttered, comfortable, impersonal spaces. No personal photos on the walls or tables. Yes, there were towels and toiletries in the bath, but they did not look like they had been used or "belonged" to anyone before. You would have checked right back out if they had!

This is the exact feeling you want in your home each and every day – you never know when there might be a showing and you never know when that showing will be the ultimate buyer.

PROFESSIONAL BONUS TIP:

I know that it is hard to keep a home tidy when you have children, especially their toys. It is essential during the selling process to have the toys limited to one area and minimized to a few containers. Not everybody has children and most do not care about the new and amazing things your new baby can do. You just cannot make a home with children turn into a children's house and expect it to sell.

The 15 Minute Clean Up

Do you have 15 minutes a day to increase the value of your house? Sure you do! Find it by getting up a little bit earlier or not watching the last half of the evening news or any of a number of ways.

Here are the rules to the 15 minutes clean up.

1. Have 5 boxes ready for the job. These should be stackable bins that are easy to put away and be unnoticed by the buyers. The first box is for trash, the second for returns (things that do not belong in your house but someone else's, such as a book on loan or a friend's coat), the third for donations/give aways, the fourth for put aways, and the fifth for anything that needs to be stored. The whole idea here is to put the items that our out of place into the bins and not go trudging through the house with each individual item to its proper place.

   Now, go through the house and put things into the proper bins. If you have a 2-story home, do the lower level and then do the upper level. You can get everyone in the family involved. Smaller children really love to put things into the different bins and do not mind going back and forth.

   Scan all items, and put anything that does not belong in that room in one of the boxes you created previously. If it does belong in that room, make sure it has a "home."

   When you are done, take out the garbage, put the "donate/give away" box in the car for drop-off or call for a pickup depending on what you have gathered. Take whatever is in the "put-away" box and put it where it belongs.

   By the time you have finished you will have a place for everything and everything will be in its place. If you will focus just 15 minutes each day, not thinking about it, not whining about it, not worrying about it   just DOING it – you will be able to keep your house in selling condition.

CASE STUDY

I have found that men usually have an easier time with the idea of staging than women – at least at first. There is a gap between what motivates a husband and a wife to sell a house. The man can turn it into a commodity faster than a woman can. However, do not think for one minute that it is because men do not care about the home! Once a stager gets to his personal space, like the shop or the den or the garage, watch out! Women are harder to convince overall – the man is harder to commit to those special things, like his shop or his chair.

Men also find it harder to change something for aesthetic reasons only. It is hard to explain the need to change something when they still see it as functional. In their opinion, if it still works, why change it? In this case, I explain that the quality of the product is zero when the product is now obsolete. This is a tough concept!

With both men and women, there is not necessarily an early understanding that the way you live is not the way you sell. Once explained, men understand quite quickly. But for women, it is a personal thing. I am always careful when I explain these things because I do not want to sound negative. However, to sell their home, they have to do a 180 degree turn from thinking of it as a personal, meaningful home to a commodity. Why you love your home may be different from why someone else is going to love it. When you are in it, it is yours. When you sell it, it has to be theirs. This is the main purpose of staging – not only to get people to see why they love the house, but to allow the most possible buyers to see what they will love instead of just a chosen few.

When you are selling a commodity, you are looking to get the best money in the fastest amount of time. To do so, you want to invest the least amount of money to get the highest return. My business philosophy is that I rarely recommend renovations unless it is something glaringly obvious. Even then, I would still consider the market. There are some neighborhoods that move so quickly that such renovations would simply not be needed.

What I do recommend, however, no matter where the house is located is painting. A fresh coat of paint does wonders for a place. Three or four years ago, the advice was to paint all your walls off white, but now I say minimize colors on the wall because next to scent, color has the biggest emotional response in people. I suggest neutral tones like a tan or pale, pale, pale yellow. Or choose a color that works with lots of different color schemes. An entire house with off white walls comes across as flat and flat walls will de-jazz your house. Some neutral tones will give your house a little character but still allow buyers to feel like they can work with it.

Other things I suggest that the home owner do is to fix those obvious problems. For instance, if you had a bathroom leak that is now fixed but the ceiling has a water stain, fix it! It may not have bothered you, but it will bother someone else. To them it is a big ugly stain. They will either believe that there is still a leak or that if you let this happen to your home, what else did you let happen? They need to feel that you took immaculate care of your home!

Whether you are selling a modest or an expensive home, all the staging techniques still apply. The only thing that comes into play is whether the home meets the standards of other homes in that price range. If you have a million dollar home and laminate countertops, I would suggest a change since Laminate is not in keeping with the home and what others would expect to find. I also look at oddities about the home that will make it stick out in a bad way. For instance, if you have a fabulous home with odd mantels over the fireplaces that do not match the

rest of the house, people will struggle with the feelings evoked in those rooms. The best thing to do in this case would be to change the mantels to something that fits the home.

People have a hard time visually and they get limited quickly by what someone else has already done. If a buyer walks into an emerald green room with red furniture and an animal print rug, the potential buyer will not buy the home because they do not have furniture that fits the living room due to color. They will be limited by what you have done. Or if you have a bonus room that you have turned into an office and they do not need an office, they will not see the potential of the room.

The same visual issues make selling a vacant home difficult. You need at least a minimal amount of furniture to help them visually see what will fit in the room. It is hard to walk into an empty living room and know that your sofa is going to fit. Sure, it will fit, BUT will everything else? They need guidance to see the actual size of the room. You need to beg, borrow, steal, or rent some furniture for empty rooms since we are simply not a visual society.

Occasionally I find that I will need to bring in a couple of accessories, like a huge mirror or large piece of artwork. Generally, however, I find that most people have too much stuff and I can simply use what they have in a different manner!

Nothing makes more of an impact on a room than the placement of the furniture and accessories. I have seen many rooms filled with beautiful individual items but the arrangement -- and therefore the overall feel -- diminished the elements. I have also seen rooms filled with dated and downright ugly furniture and accessories – and with the help of correct placement – the room looks amazingly good. The secret is to work with the pre-existing planes, lines, and angles of the space to create your great look. Your goal is to create a room that feels balanced, harmonious, and connected.

Many people believe that a new home will sell over a used home. This may be true in some cases, but not all. One thing that puts older homes above newer ones is that the owners have had a chance to figure out how to live there. They have specified a place to hang the brooms. They know where to store the dog food. This benefits the new owners because they will not have to think about it. Bring this into play! If you have figured out that the best place for the ironing board is behind the door, then keep it there and let them see the benefit of knowing where to put it before they even move in!

Many of my clients say, "I wish we had done this from the beginning. I wish we had known about staging before we got started. Will you come to Florida to decorate our new home?" The reason I hear these kinds of statements so often is because staging works.

Weekly Updates

You have cleaned and uncluttered. You have scrubbed and packed. And you have breathed a sigh of relief that it is all done. And yet – it is not all done because you have to keep it maintained. I just discussed how to keep the home looking tidy, but what about keeping it clean?

Keeping your home clean should not require a lot of work because you have already done all the hard work. Here is a list of things you should do each week to keep your home sparkling.

- Dust and vacuum at least once a week.
- Look for fingerprints on the windows, doors, walls, switch plates, and woodwork.
- Scrub the bathrooms. This means to really scrub it like it is the first time. Bathrooms have to be as clean as a motels and that will not happen with a quick swipe of a cloth.
- Mow your lawn, pull the weeds, deadhead the flowers, and trim the bushes. If it is winter and you live where it snows, you should keep your walks and driveway shoveled.
- Wipe down any lawn furniture.
- Clean and maintain your pool or spa.
- Change out any fresh cut flowers in the house or any cut greenery.

Keep the Odors at Bay

Odors have a way of finding their way back into your home. You do, after all, still live there. There are a few simple measures that will help you keep those odors at bay.

- Cook simple meals that do not require frying or ethnic spices.
- If you have kept your pets with you and not sent them on vacation to live with a friend or relative, be sure to have them groomed on a regular basis. And do not forget to change the litter box every day.
- Burn a candle that has the smell of baked goods. Cinnamon and pumpkin are good choices.

One Seller's Feelings

Here is what one seller had to say about selling their home:

> Our house lists on Monday. Today, a photographer came in to take some pretty pictures for the marketing materials, so we were madly rushing around until the last minute this morning making sure everything was still in its place.
>
> One of the things realtors always tell you do when you are selling a house is to "depersonalize" every room. This means putting away pictures and mementos that might remind someone looking at your home that it is, well, *your home.* It is not hard to depersonalize, although sometimes you have to find something impersonal to replace a personal item where the lack would be ugly.
>
> So our house is just about depersonalized; I do keep seeing things that I have forgotten to put away, but it is pretty much done. Our realtor calls this making our home look like a model home, where someone can easily imagine themselves living.
>
> Unfortunately, it also makes the house sort of hollow – at least for my family since we are used to living here and not just 'staying here.' So many of my favorite things are put away. I no longer see my Grandmother's happy face on my refrigerator door; the stacks of books that we usually live among are either gone or stashed away; even my jewelry boxes are hidden. We are presenting a model home to prospective buyers, yes, but consequently, we are having to *live* in that model home   a space lacking our familiar touches.
>
> Oh, sure, the furniture and the art are still ours, as is the Tiffany vase we got for our wedding, and my Grandfather's antique buffet. The clothes hanging in the closet, the CDs and movies

and books on the bookshelves are all ours, too. But everything feels caged up, forced into straight lines and intentional symmetry, and something about it makes me sad.

Our house looks beautiful and, despite how I feel, it *does* exude warmth and comfort. Objectively, I know these things. But for me, the beauty of our home is in the casual lived-in aura of unread magazines haphazardly strewn on the coffee table, and in the $5 black-and-white photos we buy from the picture guy in the downtown bars, and in Easter cards on the mantle.

I will be glad when we sell our home, because it is the next step for us, but I suspect I will be sad, too. We are already moving out, in a way.

PROFESSIONAL BONUS TIP:

Every morning, make sure your house is staged and ready to be shown. I suggest getting up 15 to 30 minutes earlier than normal to be sure that this is done.

Living in a Home for Sale TIPS

289. Remember how your mother told you to make your bed each day? That was great practice for staging your home. Never leave the house in the morning without first making your bed.
290. Pick up your clothes and tidy your room each morning.
291. Wet towels from the morning shower should be tossed in the dryer before you head off to work.
292. Wash the dishes and take out the trash every night.
293. Do not cook smelly food in your house while it is for sale. This includes deep fat fryers. People do not think about it, but these smells linger!

294. Do not move around the furniture to accommodate your need to watch TV or other pursuits unless you absolutely, positively put it back exactly as you found it.

295. Wipe down everything after use – this includes the stove, the microwave, countertops in the bathroom and kitchen, tables, kitchen chairs (especially if you have children), and any else that no longer looks perfectly clean.

296. If you use it, put it away! This will keep the tidying process down to a minimum.

297. Men, are you listening? Put the toilet seat down after each use. And women – this means the outer lid as well!

298. Wipe down the shower and tub each morning and put away all your personal grooming items – preferably in a tote of some kind that is put away into one of the cabinets or drawers.

299. Do not forget to check the lawn! Children's toys and lawn equipment need to be put away neatly into the garage or shed.

300. Do your laundry daily or at least every other day to keep it from building up in a pile. No one wants to see or smell your dirty clothes.

301. Do not leave your valuables – jewelry, money, and important personal papers – in your house during the sale process. Keep them with a friend or in a safety deposit box.

Sample Staging...

Conclusion

Your home is one of, if not, THE biggest asset that you possess. Therefore, you need to understand the importance of marketing your home as a showcase that appeals to the buyer and rises above the competition.

As you know, your home becomes a house a product for sale. Staging your property gives you a more competitive edge in today's market by transforming it into a marketable product. A staged property helps you sell your investment for top dollar and is the first line of defense over lowering the price. Do not settle for less at the closing table simply because you did not understand the value of staging or did not want to take the time or spend the money to do it properly.

Marketing the home for sale is key and the marketing begins with staging, whether it is new construction or resale. However, be sure that you do not nickel and dime yourself to death with updating, while missing the right time to sell. Timing and staging must go hand in hand.

In this world of busy buyers, a property has to be staged to appeal to the their imagination. They want to be able to look at your home and know that they can live there. They want to know that their furniture will fit. They want to know that everything is in "move in" condition. That is why staging is so important. It allows buyers to imagine themselves living in your home with their stuff, not yours.

Presentation is everything and staging is presentation! The result is improved functionality and complementary space. Following the techniques in this book will maximize your equity while reducing the market time for your home.

Staging works and it will work for you.

CASE STUDY

There are six things that affect the sale of your house. Two you can do nothing about: location and the market. Two need to be discussed with your realtor: price and terms. Two are solely your responsibility: condition and staging and at times, these two can happen simultaneously. These six keys are the main ingredients in any sale. That is why staging gives your property such an edge. The recipe for success is helping a buyer sell in any market by controlling what can be controlled.

It is essential to understand that staging a home is an investment and not a cost. Minimal changes will get you more money. Home sellers that have had their home on the market too long will start dropping their price, often in increments of $10,000 to $20,000 per pop. Staging a home is a fraction of that.

In today's market, where older homes can sit a long time without being sold, staging is a necessity and not an option. In fact, in any market, if you want your house to the top choice for an interested buyer, you really have no choice.

When it comes to vacant properties, forgoing staging can mean forgoing the sale. Vacant homes are cold. They do not give the buyer the warm fuzzy feeling they are looking for. For most people, staging an entire vacant home is too costly, but there are key rooms that really need attention. These include the kitchen, dining room or eat-in area, all bathrooms, and the master bedroom and bath. Depending upon the budget, you might also consider lightly staging a family room or living room.

Many people will say, "But my house is not getting any showings. Why should I stage my home if no one is going to see it?" My answer is photos. Most buyers look on the Internet to do their initial research. Homes that have not been staged do not photograph well. Staging your home and taking new photos is a great way to start getting those showings!

Sellers see their house through their own eyes and believe that it is showing well – whether it is currently lived in or currently vacant. The problem is that sellers are emotionally attached. They see far more than a house – they remember a home. A stager can help sell a home faster and for more money because we can stand back and see the house and the potential it has to offer to the next owner.

Stagers, along with your realtor, can help you sort out the condition of your home and determine what renovations may be needed to get you more money. These renovations need to be kept to a minimum and be profitable.

When it comes to repairs and refreshing, lightening and brightening are my two words. Paint is cheap. Less than $100 for some paint can increase a sale by $1000. If someone offered you a 10% increase on your return at the bank, you would take it!

Besides lightening and brightening, there is cleaning and uncluttering. One of the most overlooked cleaning projects is the front yard! Landscaping truly counts. Look at your trees and bushes. Are they covering the house? As any realtor knows, if you cannot see it, you cannot sell it!

All this said, it is important to keep things in proportion to the home. There is no need to add amenities to a home that go beyond the neighborhood. This is even true of landscaping! Adding an expensive Japanese garden will cause potential buyers to take notice, but it will not cause them to pay for the renovation!

When staging, you also have to keep things in proportion. You must use props that fit. And you must know the weaknesses and strengths of the home. Every home has them. In fact, I often recommend that a seller sit down and write a 60 second commercial about their house. I ask them what they would talk about if they had just one minute to tell me about their house. This will bring often bring out the features that attracted them to the house – the same ones that will attract the buyer. Staging is a way to emphasize these strengths.

What do customers have to say about staging? "This is the best investment I could have ever made. It really blew me away."

Appendix 1

Room-By-Room Cleaning Checklist

☝ **PROFESSIONAL BONUS TIP:**

Everything needs to be "Q Tip Clean" – clean to the point that you do not see any piece of dust or dirt.

Kitchen

1. Let cleansers do the scrubbing for you! Spray your oven with cleaner the night before you plan to deep clean your kitchen, literally marinating the grease and grime, making it simple to sponge off.

2. Vacuum stove vents, refrigerator coils, floor, and counters.

3. Defrost that freezer. A blow-drier aimed at the ice will speed up the process.

4. Get rid of old foods and those jars of things you thought you would like but never ate.

5. Wash out the trashcan and spray it with a good disinfectant before putting in a new lining.

Bathrooms

1. Spray shower and tub with strong cleanser.

2. Pour cleaner into the toilet bowl, and spray the outside with the same cleaner. Let the chemicals do the cleaning while you do the next steps

3. Clean mirrors, chrome, bathroom scale, and light fixtures with glass cleaner.

4. Vacuum everything. This will remove dust and hair that is so hard to get up when surfaces are wet.

5. Empty and clean the wastepaper basket.

6. Clean the sink and wipe off the cleanser you already applied to the shower and tub.

7. Working from the top of the toilet down, clean the outside, and brush and flush the inside.

8. Scrub the floor with a strong cleanser. Tough tile floors can be most easily cleaned by hand with the scrub-brush side of a bathroom-only sponge.

9. One more tip: spaghetti mops are more efficient at getting into tough corners than sponge mops. Many types can even be thrown in the washing machine between cleanings.

Living Room

1. Dust and vacuum corners and crevices from high points to low. Remember dust falls downward so you want to clean from the top to the bottom of any room.

2. Vacuum furniture, lampshades, and pictures. Remember all those gadgets that come with your vacuum cleaner? Use them here, and experiment with different attachments for furniture and corners of rooms.
3. Vacuum or wash curtains.
4. Dust wood furniture.
5. Dust mop floors.
6. Vacuum carpet.
7. Take plants outside for a gentle washing with a fine spray from your garden hose. Plants and their pots get dusty over the winter.

Bedrooms

1. Wash, or dry-clean curtains.
2. Take blinds outside and wash them.
3. Strip bed linens and dust ruffle.
4. Polish wood furniture and dust knickknacks.
5. Vacuum everything, from the floor behind and under the bed to the carpet, lampshade, and pictures.
6. Clean mirrors and wipe down light fixtures and lamps.
7. Dust mop wood floors.

Sample Staging...

Appendix 2

Preparing Your Home For Sale Checklists

Exterior Checklist

1. Touch up trim paint on doors, window frames, fascia, etc.

2. If your lawn shows no signs of life, a little fertilizer and some water will do wonders for its color.

3. Overgrown shrubbery should be cut back to show as much of the exterior as possible.

4. A low-cost investment in seasonal flowers or ground cover will add a personal touch.

5. Weed and then mulch all planting areas.

6. Replace missing shutters, gutters, and downspouts and remove any debris.

7. Inspect the roof for necessary repairs and any visible broken shingles or tiles.

8. Fix cracks in the driveway and clean excessive stains.

9. Fences should be mended and painted.

10. If a street sweeper does not come every week, make sure the area in front of your curb and driveway are clear of debris. Wash it down with the hose.

11. Wash all windows inside and outside.

12. Go around the perimeter of the house and move all garbage cans, discarded wood scraps, and extra building materials. Throw away those scraps and extra materials. Put the garbage cans in the garage.

13. Clear patios or decks of all small items such as small planters, flowerpots, charcoal, barbecues, and toys. Put them in a storage unit.

Living Area Check list

1. Clean your home from top to bottom.

2. Repair any cracks or holes in walls and touch-up paint.

3. Doors should be cleaned and touched-up as well. All torn screens should be repaired or replaced.

4. Have carpeting and draperies cleaned.

5. If you have a fireplace, make sure all tile is in good condition, the screen is in good shape, and the hearth is clean.

6. Lubricate squeaking doors, windows, and cabinets.

7. Store out-of-season clothes so closets do not look cluttered.

8. Pre-pack items, which may clutter your home and make rooms appear smaller.

Kitchen Checklist

1. Keep the counters clean and clear of appliances. All appliances should be clean and neatly organized. An open appearance with sunlight and green plants here and there will make the room a focal point. Make it light and bright.

2. Clean and wax the kitchen floor. If the floor looks old and dull, consider replacing the flooring.

3. Clean fans and vent hoods.

Bathroom Checklist

1. All bathroom appliances should be thoroughly cleaned. Remove stains from sinks, toilets, and bathtubs.

2. Replace old caulking around bathtub and sinks.

3. Repair or replace leaky faucets.

4. Unclog and sanitize drains to remove odors.

5. Clean all mirrors.

Garage, Basement, and Attic Checklist

1. Have a garage sale to dispose of any unwanted items. Family heirlooms, which you will take with you, should be boxed and stored in the garage until you move.

2. Degreasers are available at your local home repair store to remove stains from the garage floor.

3. Remove any cobwebs.

4. If the basement or attic is a functioning part of the house, make sure the area is clean and in good repair.

Showing Your Home Checklist

1. Dust and vacuum the whole house thoroughly.

2. Lightly clean and straighten up living areas.

3. Open all drapes and blinds to let in as much light as possible. Turn on lamps and other lights as necessary to brighten each room.

4. Any household or children's items should be stored away. This includes toys, bikes, skateboards, etc.

5. Turn television sets off. Turn on a radio with soft music at low volume.

6. While your home is being held open, arrange to spend the time away from the house, especially if you have small children.

7. Keep pets away from potential buyers and keep pet areas clean.

8. Try baking chocolate chip cookies or brownies just before the open house. A pleasant aroma means home to many people.

Appendix 3

How to Clean Common Household Fabrics

PROFESSIONAL BONUS TIP:

The smelliest room in your house next to the bathroom is the living room because it has the most fabric and fabric absorbs odors.

For deep cleaning, the proper method depends largely on the type of fabric. Consult the chart below.

Plain-weave linen and cotton including canvas, chintz, denim, gingham, sailcloth, sateen, ticking, and toile: Curtains, slipcovers, and other removable items are cold-water machine washable, so long as they are preshrunk and colorfast. Test by rubbing a wet white washcloth gently on a discreet area, such as a hidden seam, to see if any color comes off. For major cleaning, hire a professional. Glazed fabrics, such as chintz, should never be ironed because heat damages the shiny finish.

Silk and Satin, including crepe and taffeta: These fabrics should be dry-cleaned. Satin, which can be woven from pure silk, rayon, acetate, or polyester, has a lustrous face and a dull underside; iron only the dull side. (Harsh sunlight is the enemy of silk, so if used for draperies, it should be lined with a cotton backing; position silk-upholstered furniture out of direct sunlight, or protect it with cotton slipcovers.)

Rayon: Although rayon itself is washable, it is often sized with coatings that are water-soluble; professional cleaning is best unless a care tag directs otherwise.

Jacquards including brocade, damask, matelassé, and tapestry: Any such pattern, which is created by the weave, requires mild washing. For cotton and linen, use the gentle cycle on the washing machine. If the fabric contains silk, dry-clean only. Before laundering, mend, clip, or point out any loose threads to a professional cleaner.

Pile fabrics including chenille, corduroy, velvet, and velveteen: If made of preshrunk cotton, these can be washed with water and detergent (test for colorfastness as with plain weaves). Avoid snags, which can destroy construction. Fabrics with pile made of acetate, polyester, or rayon should be professionally cleaned. In either case, do not iron, because piles flatten easily from moisture and pressure.

Wool: Dry-clean only. When vacuuming, be careful not to rub vigorously since wool is difficult to repair or patch once it is torn.

Appendix 4

How to Remove Specific Stains

The diluted dishwashing-soap solution called for below is made with one tablespoon of fragrance- and dye-free liquid soap (containing sodium laurel sulfate, or sodium laureth sulfate) and nine and a half ounces of water. Pour it into a tiny spray bottle.

Do not use the enzyme detergent, called for below, on protein fibers, such as silk, wool, cashmere, or angora.

Always wash fabric after using a dry solvent (such as mineral spirits or acetone), and do not use acetone on acetate.

Grease including butter, oil, and mayonnaise: Treat area with a dry solvent (such as mineral spirits or acetone) in a well-ventilated room. Using an eyedropper, rinse with isopropyl alcohol; dry well. Spray diluted dishwashing-soap solution on any remaining residue, and soak the item in an enzyme detergent before washing.

Fruit or vegetable including juice and jam: Spray diluted dishwashing-soap solution on the stain to remove sugars. Using an eyedropper, flush the area with white vinegar and then hydrogen peroxide to remove any remaining color. Follow with an enzyme detergent to remove residue before washing.

Red Wine: Spray diluted dishwashing-soap solution on stain; tamp with a soft-bristled brush. Flush with water, apply white vinegar, and tamp; let stand several minutes; flush again. If stain remains, apply hydrogen peroxide and let stand. If stain persists, apply one or two drops of ammonia to wet area. Flush with water. Treat with an enzyme detergent; wash. If stain is still there, apply powdered, non-chlorinated color-safe bleach, such as sodium percarbonate; rewash.

Coffee or tea: Using an eyedropper, flush area with lemon juice or white vinegar to remove stain; then treat with stronger bleach, if necessary. To help remove sugar or milk, spray area with diluted dishwashing-soap solution, then wash with an enzyme detergent.

Lipstick: Use a dull-edged knife to remove excess lipstick. Using an eyedropper, apply a dry solvent (such as mineral spirits or acetone) in a well-ventilated room; tamp with a soft-bristled brush. Flush area with isopropyl alcohol and tamp. Repeat until all stain is removed, and let dry. Spray with diluted dishwashing-soap solution. Treat with an enzyme detergent, and wash.

Mustard: Using an eyedropper, flush stain with vinegar; then wash with diluted dishwashing-soap solution.

Soy Sauce: Spray with diluted dishwashing-soap solution; tamp with a soft-bristled brush. Flush with water, apply white vinegar, and tamp; let stand several minutes, and flush again. If stain remains, apply hydrogen peroxide, and let stand. If stain persists, apply one or two drops of ammonia to wet area. Flush with water. Treat with an enzyme detergent; wash. If stain is still there, apply a powdered non-chlorinated color-safe bleach, such as sodium percarbonate; rewash.

Felt tip ink: First, build a "dam" around stain with mineral oil or petroleum jelly. Always work within the confines of the dam. Test the ink with a cotton swab saturated with water and another one saturated with isopropyl alcohol to determine whether the ink is oil-based or water-based. Whichever solvent pulls more pigment out of the stain is the one that should be used. If isopropyl alcohol is more effective, follow the steps for ballpoint ink stains below. If water is more effective, spray the stain with diluted dishwashing-soap solution, and then flush with cold water.

Mud: If stain is a combination of mud and grass, treat grass stain first. (See grass, above.) Shake or scrape off residue; pre-treat stain with diluted dishwashing-soap solution and soak. Then treat with an enzyme detergent; wash.

Protein including blood and eggs: Spray diluted dishwashing-soap solution on stain, and let it sit; rinse in tepid water. If stain remains, treat area with an enzyme detergent, and wash according to label instructions.

Grass: Treat area with a dry solvent in a well-ventilated room. Press with cheesecloth; tamp with a soft-bristled brush. Repeat to remove as much pigment as possible. Flush area with isopropyl alcohol, tamp, and let dry. Follow up with an enzyme detergent to remove residue before washing.

White wine: Flush the stain with cold water and spray with diluted dishwashing-soap solution. Treat area with an enzyme detergent and then wash.

Chocolate: Gently scrape off excess chocolate; spray area with diluted dishwashing-soap solution. Follow up with an enzyme detergent to remove residue before washing.

Wax or gum: Use ice to freeze wax or gum or place item in the freezer; scrape or crack off as much as you can, then remove residue with an oil solvent or mineral spirits. Rinse with isopropyl alcohol; let dry. Treat with an enzyme detergent; wash.

Sauces including tomato, ketchup, and barbeque: Scrape off sauce; spray area with diluted dishwashing-soap solution. Soak in tepid water. If color remains, apply white vinegar with an eyedropper. Treat with an enzyme detergent; wash. If color persists, apply several drops of hydrogen peroxide; let sit. Rinse; treat again with enzyme detergent, and wash.

Vinaigrette: First, treat stain as a grease stain. (See grease, above.) Then flush with white vinegar to remove any remaining spot. Follow with an enzyme detergent to remove residue before washing.

Ballpoint ink: Build a "dam" around the stain with mineral oil or petroleum jelly. Always work within the confines of the dam. Treat area with isopropyl alcohol using an eyedropper. Remove any remaining pigment with a dry solvent in a well-ventilated room; let dry. Rinse with diluted dishwashing-soap solution; then wash with an enzyme detergent in warm water.

Appendix 5

Glossary of Terms

APPRAISAL – A written estimate and opinion of value; a conclusion resulting from the analysis of facts.

APPRAISER – One qualified by education, training, and experience who is hired to estimate the value of real and personal property based upon experience, judgment, facts, and the use of the formal appraisal processes.

CLUTTER – Household and personal "stuff" falling into one of four categories: 1. No longer used or loved, 2. Things that are disorganized, 3. Too much in too little space, 4. Things that are not finished.

COMPARABLE – Properties listed in an appraisal report that are substantially equivalent to the subject property, comparable in selling price, rental, income or similar measure.

CONDOMINIUM – Fee ownership of a unit in multi-unit building with joint ownership of common areas.

DEADHEAD – Removing the dead blooms off of flowering plants so that they will continue to grow and flower.

UNCLUTTER – An industry term that means to get rid of a confused or disordered state or collection, AKA uncluttered.

DEPERSONALIZE – Make impersonal or present home as an object for sale by getting rid of all personal items such as photos, trophies, souvenirs, etc.

DRESSING TO SELL – Another name for getting a home ready to sell.

FLYLADY – An excellent resource to learn how to clean and stay clutter-free (**www.flylady.net**)

FREECYCLE – A resource that can help you eliminate your unwanted items locally (**www.freecycle.org**).

FSBO (For Sale by Owner) – When a seller wishes to sell their home by themselves.

HARDSCAPE – Refers to the paved areas and other non-living landscaping features.

HGTV (Home and Garden TV) – Home & Garden Television, better known as HGTV, is a cable television network in the U.S. and Canada. Programming consists of numerous home and garden improvement, maintenance, renovation, and remodeling shows.

HOME PRESENTATION – Preparing your home in a way that it shows well for sale.

HOME STAGER – Home Stager is a consultant who provides advice and services in presenting properties to ensure a sale. Home Stagers know which rooms to concentrate on, what effects to use to make a room "feel' better, and how to spend a little money wisely to get the best return on your investment.

HOME STAGING – The process of preparing any home for sale, regardless of price or location.

HOUSE FLUFFING – Home staging is also called home enhancement or property enhancement. On the east coast they sometimes call it home fluffing.

LANDSCAPE – The visible features of an area of land, including physical elements such as landforms, living elements of flora and fauna, and abstract elements such as lighting and weather conditions.

MARKET PRICE – The price paid regardless of pressures, motives, or intelligence.

MARKET VALUE – The price at which a willing seller would sell and a willing buyer would buy, neither being under abnormal pressure.

OFFER – A promise by one party to act in a certain manner provided the other party will act in the manner requested. The offeror is the one who makes the offer to the offeree.

REAL ESTATE AGENT – A person with a state/provincial license to represent a buyer or a seller in a real-estate transaction in exchange for commission. Most agents work for a real-estate broker or realtor.

REALTOR – A service mark used for a real-estate agent affiliated with the National Association of Realtors.

REALTY – A term sometimes used as a collective noun for real property or real estate.

REDESIGNER – Someone who prepares your home for sale using staging techniques and only your furniture and accessories.

SCHWARTZ, BARB – The founder of **www.stagedhomes.com** and the person who coined the term Stage in the '70s.

Bibliography

About.com. "Home Staging Myths." 2015.
http://homestaging.about.com/od/hs/tp/5-Home-Staging-Myths.htm.

Christian, Vicki, ed. *Designed to Sell: Smart Ideas That Pay Off.*
Des Moines, Iowa: Meredith Books, 2006.

DIY Network. Scripps Network, Inc. September 28, 2006
http://www.diynetwork.com.

Ebizmba.com. "Top Most Popular Real Estate Web Sites." 2015.
http://www.ebizmba.com/articles/real-estate-websites.

FlyLady.net. FlyLady and Company, Inc. September 28, 2006 **http://www.flylady.net.**

Gardenresearch.com. "Garden Market Research." 2013. **www.gardenresearch.com/index.php?q=show&id=3737.**

Glink, Ilyce R. *50 Simple Steps You Can Take to Sell Your Home Faster and for More Money in Any Market.* New York: Three Rivers Press, 2003.

HGTV. Home. Ideas. Life. Scripps Network, Inc. September 28, 2006 **http://www.hgtv.com.**

Houselogic.com. "Evaluate Your House for Basement Finishing." 2015. **http://www.houselogic.com/home-advice/basements/evaluate-your-house-basement-finishing/.**

Houselogic.com. "Smart Options: Basement Flooring." 2015. **http://www.houselogic.com/home-advice/basements/smart-options-basement-flooring/.**

Irwin, Robert. *Improve the Value of Your Home Up to $100,000: 50 Surefire Techniques and Strategies.* Hoboken, New Jersey: John Wiley and Sons, 2003.

Lankarge, Vicki and Daniel J. Nahorney. *How to Increase the Value of Your Home.* New York: McGraw-Hill, 2005.

Lowes.com. "Remove Old Wallpaper." 2015. **http://www.lowes.com/projects/paint-stain-and-wallpaper/remove-old-wallpaper/project.**

Marketwatch.com. "New Survey Finds Small Décor Changes in Your Home can Affect Your Mood." 2013. **http://www.marketwatch.com/story/new-survey-finds-small-decor-changes-in-your-home-can-affect-your-mood-2013-09-26.**

Realtor.org. "2014 Profile of Home Buyers and Sellers." 2014. **http://www.realtor.org/sites/default/files/reports/2014/2014-profile-of-home-buyers-and-sellers-highlights.pdf.**

Remodeling.hw.net. "2014 Cost vs. Value Report." 2015. **http://www.remodeling.hw.net/cost-vs-value/2014/.**

Remodeling.hw.net. 2014 Cost vs. Value Report: Trends." 2015. **http://www.remodeling.hw.net/cost-vs-value/2014/trends.**

Stagedhomes.com. "ASP Home Staging Statistics." 2015. **http://www.stagedhomes.com/mediacenter/stagingstatistics.php.**

USnews.com. "How much will that Patio or Deck Cost? 2014. **http://money.usnews.com/money/personal-finance/articles/2014/06/30/how-much-will-that-patio-or-deck-cost.**

Webb, Martha and Sarah Parsons Zackheim. *Dress Your House for Success: 5 Fast Steps to Selling Your House, Apartment, or Condo for the Highest Possible Price.* New York: Three Rivers Press,1997.

Wikihow.com. "How to Get and Maintain a Healthy Lawn." 2015. **http://www.wikihow.com/Get-and-Maintain-a-Healthy-Lawn.**

Wikipedia: The Free Encyclopedia. Wikimedia Foundation. September 28, 2006 **http://en.wikipedia.org.**

Index